AF710052

THE DAWN OF SATISFACTION

A Foundation of Understanding

by

Bill Huth

High Sierra Books

Gold Beach, OR 97444

Copyright 2001 High Sierra Books
All rights reserved

ISBN: 0-9715482-0-X
LCCN: 2001094324

Copies available from:
HIGH SIERRA BOOKS
34010 Ophir Road
Gold Beach, OR 97444
Fax: 541-247-5375

FORWARD

The Dawn Of Satisfaction is Bill Huth's latest victory in a lifelong battle to understand, invent, and implement methods and means in which hard science and metaphysics converge to produce a world view that promotes racial, social, natural, and scientific unity while at the same time holding individuality in high esteem. The stringent rubrics of science, however fruitful in recent centuries, have failed to satisfy a fundamental instinct inherent in humankind's biological/mental structure. For an individual to be whole, to be connected to the primal unity that is the glue of the universe, the spiritual component of human psychology must be satisfied. On the other hand, to sacrifice scientific advances of the recent centuries in the name of a remote and unsubstantiated deity has proven to be of greatest advantage to politicians and pedagogues. Religious myths, for all intents and purposes, rarely satisfy the individual need for spirituality. Instead these myths support and protect secular hierarchies with political aspirations. In an attempt to cross the seemingly unbridgeable chasm between scientific determinism and mysticism, Huth has devised a unique dialectic that synthesizes the two into a new, life affirming philosophy.

Drawing on scientific theory, especially those concerned with evolution, and religious scripture from around the world, Huth has hammered out a new way of thinking that surpasses that which came before it. In the traditions of

Heraclitus and Nietzsche, he has paved the way to overcoming the fears of living a purely mechanized existence along with the horrors an eternal hell and a heaven that serves no purpose — an eternity of listless boredom. In short, if digested slowly and with proper meditation, Huth offers his readers a heaven on earth, an eternity of purpose which exposes the god in the machine. Although many may think Huth's approach radical, Galileo, the ideal inductive research worker, rejected Kepler's theory that the tides were due to the moon's attraction as an "occult fancy". Grounded in scientific bedrock, Huth's theories are far from occult meanderings such as those espoused by Cornelius Agrippa and Carlos Castaneda. Huth's theories hold water under the scrutiny of scientific method and, in the end, will not be ignored.

The recent discoveries of "black matter" and "black energy" have sent many (but not all) astrophysicists back to the drawing board. In a recent article in *Time* magazine (June 25, 2001), an article entitled *How The Universe Will End* claimed to have solved the biggest mystery in the cosmos through the aforementioned discoveries: the universe will continue to expand until it runs out of gas and then simply cease to be. In other words, all is for naught. For Huth, because the existence of *all*, from the subatomic particle to the Milky Way Galaxy, is the self-expression of a Universal Mind, the universe ceasing to be is like God committing suicide. A proponent of Bergson's *Creative Evolution*, Huth realizes that the concept of nothing is a logical fallacy. The universe ceasing to be is an occult fancy.

Huth's matrix of existence unfolds to encompass both eternity and the moment. Because we are self-expressions of a Universal Mind, death is a concept supported only by the limitations of human senses. Although difficult to grasp in the context of these few pages, one may recall the words of Socrates, "An unexamined life is not worth living," and equate it to the Universal Mind. This entity, which Huth painstakingly analyzes from a scientific standpoint, is attempting self-realization through physical existence. The absence of physical existence in no way negates the Universal Mind, and the presence of physical existence cannot define the Universal Mind. The two, physical existence and that which guides its "groping forward", are one and the same and yet separate. I am an indivudual and I am a fragment, just as all physicality, of the Universal Mind; I am an individual part of the whole, just as a liver cell is an individual part of my body. We are one. This is the cornerstone of Huth's philosophy.

For students of Mazdaism and Jungian psychology, this may sound familiar. Huth, however, pushes beyond the bounds of these recognized schools of thought into uncharted waters. What he finds on his voyage is fascinating, inspiring, and terrifying. In following Huth's thought, one must take on a new kind of responsibility, a responsibility in which "love thy neighbor" takes on new meaning and evolution becomes a duty and not a purely mechanistic process. To deny Huth's philosophy also takes courage: the virus, refusing to acknowledge its connection to the host, either annihilates the host or is destroyed by the host's defense system. In either case, readers of Huth's work are bound to reexamine their place in the universe. In the end, this is what it's all about.

John Gist

A WORD FROM THE AUTHOR

When I decided to use the title *The Dawn Of Satisfaction* for my next book, involved with evolution, I never realized how satisfied I should be. Seventy-six years old, a family, millions of dollars in assets, good health. And that's not all. Through the efforts of billions who were born before me, I have been able to research, through science and nature, a foundation for my existence, which provides a future forever.

This foundation, naturally, involves the science of biology, and biology's devotion to nature, and the functioning of life. After swaying to the left, my beliefs welcomed the words of Darwin and the thoughts of philosophers. I was also infatuated by various authors of many religious societies. King Solomon, in the Old Testament, spoke of the comparison of man to beast in his book *Ecclesiastes* (3:18-22), my first ever acknowledgment of a real relationship of man to animal in the Good Books. However, mythology remained but never held any rank in my mentality. Fanciful thinking, which probably came first, undoubtedly holds a position in our mental make-up. However, its rank is limited today as child's play. The various philosophers connected with religious thought spoke many mental reflections of nature. Mythical and natural observations were tediously entwined to present others with a solution or conclusion of what the results of living would present.

What else could living present than living? Living can only mean living. Eternity is a description of timelessness. Timelessness could never compare to existence except through evolutionary progress. Living is a process of accomplishment. In fact, living is accomplishments just as evolution is described as a natural process of improvement through experience.

The Dawn Of Satisfaction might be considered as the brink of understanding. Philosophy is described as the study of knowledge. Philosophy explains the language that is used to study knowledge. Knowledge is as close as we can get to truth.

Knowledge never presents any excuse.

Bill Huth, 2001

BELIEF

All creatures are led down many trails by the leaders of their species. Yet, though there is an unending supply of routes to travel, the ones that lead to truth seem to be the simplest to follow. To return to a split in the highway requires only relaxation, to continue once again requires faith.

Satisfaction will render itself just as dissatisfaction will prove its worth. Both will be instruments of achievement. The flux of determination will exterminate doubt. All tribal instinct will succumb to exaltation. Only basic being will blend. Satisfaction conceived as equality Becomes through egalitarianism of All Creation.

When silence wins out, humanity will hang its head in shame for believing to be the leaders of All Creation.

Eternity is a natural position for all life.

It has been a continuous challenge that Mind has been engaged in since the thought of Being first sparked life. To Be had no exact meaning when desire of Mind first entertained this thought, and Being was offered in a broad spectrum, yet motivation was far beyond any desire. To merely Be was sufficient as life first produced. To Be would fill the container. With this limitation of Being, a rapacious self-acknowledgement came into play. Mind must sacrifice Its seclusion and cooperatively guide that which It had created to Be. To Be had overwhelmed Its capacitron. Just as the creation of Frankenstein, life was on the loose. The flux of intelligence was now beyond the control of Its instigator. Mind was now forced to Be as a Partner rather than a dominator — part physical and part etheric mentality.

To Be exposed Mind in Its most precious state. Willing to sacrifice a part of Its own to create what might Be explained as companionship. Something to Be with. The design, in the Beginning, had to satisfy Itself. There were none to compare nor complain. Nature was to Become as a satisfaction to Itself, through the desire of Mind. Mind, Being without physical, ponderable, materialism was to gaze upon that which only desire must contrive. The complete mental state of Mind, through Its aspiration sensed association, physical Life Became. The flame of Nature was now at the side of intelligence, and joined in the evolutionary process of life.

A speck of Monera, as Haeckel might describe It.

Perhaps an Atom through the eyes of Einstein. Or something beyond the eye, and only seen in the sense of Mind, Life Began to Evolutionize. One step beyond Imagination. Intelligence was now in the hands of satisfaction.

Upon transformation of any Being, the flesh and bones of the mundane, through the process of consumption and decomposition, are presented as other Beings through the process of Birth.

Mind remains and continues to flow through Eternal Matter as this Matter transforms into bodies of the future, and reacts through Mind as a Cosmic Force.

The accomplishments and reflections of all Beings continue to be relayed by Mind as others who are effected by the accomplishments of former Beings carry on in Life.

Those transpired now live through Mind and reap the benefits of all who live through this energy of the evolutionary Mind/Being.

Design, as a thought, proves the direction Mind is perpetually traveling.

I have danced around the word soul for most of my life. Originally my soul was going to be my way of getting into heaven. However, when I was told my pets could not go to heaven, I really didn't care about going there myself.

As years passed by, the thought of heaven grew weaker and weaker, and the final belief I settled for was: heaven is impossibility.

My use of the word soul during the years had changed to sole. Sole being the outside covering of all animate and/or inanimate life. This word "sole" explained things as good as "soul" except during the frustrating times of speech. Like a lot of other words, the meaning had to be defined by the context of the thought.

Today I first used the word organ to replace sole or soul. Organ is a common word that explains all parts of life that exist on earth and throughout the Universal Atmosphere of Space. An organ can be thought of as any mechanism or machine of life, or for life. It covers the atom to the ultimate. One organ contains many other organs. In fact, the Organ of Being could contain every concept of life. A way in which many look at God.

In reality there is no way of defining ourselves other than being organs. One organ has never represented itself as being better or over another organ. All organs are sponsors of other organs. Organs have no definite shape, color, or size.

In final, organs are life for All. Interchange has never been a problem.

Creative progress fuels itself through observation.

How can a person believe in evolution if they cannot believe in the equality of Universal Creation?

My mind becomes startled every time I see, read, or hear the word soul. I almost immediately put my mind in gear and look for another definition of this powerful word. I am positive I am not the only person who ever heard the line, "If you are not nice and obey the Ten Commandments, you and your soul will never go to heaven." My mother did not only speak these words to me, I heard them every time I went to Sunday school. Also, I have been told that my soul belongs to me forever, and it is my ticket to get into heaven, just as long as I remain good. Therefore, if these words are true, then, evidently, my soul looks exactly like me, even though I can't see it, and is mine forever. That is if I get into heaven. If I go to hell, both of us will be burnt up, and I will never get to see my relatives in heaven.

There is a meaning behind my soul that represents me, and I'm sure this meaning is that when I go to heaven, as I have been taught, my soul will go right along with me and will replace my body, which looks just the same. The reason for this is that my soul looks like me, so when we go to heaven the people (no dogs allowed) already will know its me. Also, the advantage for everyone else having a soul is they are easy to identify too. They tell me that all souls look like their owners (and I can't see much advantage to having one if it looked like some one else). By having a soul, each person, through this soul, which looks like them, has proof of who they are and how good they have been during their life on earth. This is all that matters for their entry into heaven. As the Bible says, "Earth is a proving grounds to get into heaven."

In my mind I feel that the word soul was spoken long before it was written, or carved on wood or stone, or scrolled on any type of matter which makes up all of Creation, animate, or inanimate. During this time mysticism, I feel, had not been originated nor was it in practice. Life itself was mystic enough, and I cannot believe our wits had produced any thoughts concerning minds, souls, spirits or devils. Life itself was problem enough — trying to survive — being eaten or beaten or caught in a giant earthquake that was being caused by the crust of the earth grinding and breaking up.

Before the advent of the Word "soul" there was another word that had a definite meaning with no strings attached. Although it was spelt in a different way, and sounded just the same, this word, "sole", was used to describe the hoof of a horse or ass. In 1440 it was the sole of a shoe. In 1418 E. E. Wills used the word sole as, "Ionet my wife kept her sole, without husband." In 1700 it was described as "an old Burly Drab (women with prostitutes for sale) that screams out the sale of her maids and their sole. It was summed up in 1615 by Crook, sole: body of man.

Etymologists say the ultimate etymology of the word soul is uncertain. However the ultimate etymology of the word sole has never been, it seems, important enough to mention in the same manner as the very mystical word soul. From the beginning of its utterance, when the word sole, which meant the covering of the bodies, was changed to mean the mythical soul of man, there has been created a question of what sole or soul really is. It could very well have been that soul or sole, both sounding the same, could have originally been used as a word to describe the shapes of all animate and inanimate parts of Creation. Research can only present theories. I can find all kinds of references to sole as meaning the sole of the foot. However, I can also see that the word sole was used, in cases, for the explanation of bodies. By the evolutionary process in which the body unfolds, I am sure with the advent of speech, and as small as our vocabulary was many thousands of years ago, humankind searched more for a sound or word to describe our physical appearance than a mythical sound to describe something that really never has been seen, or for that matter has really never existed. It would be easy to change a word that describes the physical appearance of our bodies into a word that sounded the same yet no longer meant the sole of the foot, but rather a mystic sole that had a real advantage: ETERNAL LIFE. Also, it had the powerful benefits of giving more control to those who were taking freedom from others.

Soul, which I now understand as containing the matter that makes up the body of man, was first used in this way. It was later switched to mean sole, the bottom of the feet, or as foundation for different things.

Words are of much greater value when they refer to mystical belief than when they are just plain old sounds. After thousands of years, both mystics and scientists are still groping for the proper application of the word soul to life or afterlife.

Soul seems to be many things. However, its real value seems to be a ticket to get into some afterlife where the streets are paved with gold and we live forever. Soul, as it is now spelled, seems to mean much more today than it did when the word was first uttered. It's real value seems to be where it can get us; it seems to offer us admittance to some ultra-mystical Shangri-la that has no proof of existence.

As I mentioned before, explanation of how the earth came about was not really needed. The Creationists of seven thousand years ago have their seven day story for our planet earth. Earth at that time was really no problem; earth could be seen and felt. There was no question about it. Heaven was what they really wanted to hear about in those days, something you could not see yet were told existed. This presented a problem and still does. It's for certain, these mystics tell us, we're going to be there for the rest of our lives. I can say for sure that they're scared of risking another story about something else now, something that we can't see.

Mankind, with their evolutionizing of the automobile, might be compared with the super-desire of what we explain as God as Creation continues to unfold.

Getting down to the nitty-gritty: it is really God who likes to drive in cars, and God's the one who's behind all of the comforts that are added to each new model. God lives through mankind, and all the rest of It's Universal Creation.

Accepting the proof of both physical and mental evolution does not remove the prospect of a Heaven upon transposition. Rather it presents the knowledge of a Heaven at hand. Eternity, as fact, belongs to ALL. By their acknowledging the fact that each is a part of all, and the word "death" only describes beginning, or birth of a beginning. Each has an instant of change. Not a disappearance of either, merely change. The actions of any creature are instilled in those who visualize the life which surrounds them. Life holds truth for all Creation. All Creation have digested benefits from others. Life brings about relationship; relationship has no boundaries.

If I had more of Haeckel in me, I possibly could make this explanation a little easier. In any event, I will try. Ernst Haeckel, unlike some other evolutionistic scientists, spent most of his life in the study of what I call jellyfish. To Haeckel jellyfish came with hundreds of different sizes and shapes, and he gave each a different name. Also, he devoted much of his time in studying shelled fish. These shelled animals are just as the jellyfish. Their flesh is nearly the same; it's the sole or shell that varies in shape. There are some that clamp to rocks, and some are completely covered with sole/shell and are seen in many different shapes. I have never dissected any of them, but I am sure that their fleshy bodies are even more alike than most believe. The common snail with its shell body removed looks just like a slug as we know it.

Our vessel, like sole/bodies, make up billions of our species. Each basically resembles the other, and yet color, shape, and size make a great difference in appearance. Humankind do not look alike except for standing with head, arms, hands, body, legs and feet. One might be seven feet tall and black, and another four feet tall and white with orange hair. Some have round skulls, and some have long, thin skulls. None seem to have identical finger prints.

We have a near look-alike relative, just as all Creation is related, which comes very close to the human species: the apes. The apes also have a near look alike: the monkeys. Both lack the ability to speak a complete sentence. Although they have been at the side of Creation for millions of years, and came from the same roots, the apes have never developed the ability to create a simple sentence of sounds, as mankind has. They make many sounds and expressions, yet no lengthy conversations. Undoubtedly it has to do with their physical make up. However, a parrot and those of that species can develop clear enunciation of words and are capable of learning sentences which make it possible to ask for what they desire. Most common, "Polly wants a cracker."

Was this a mistake in evolution, or was it purposely made so that humankind can speak with lengthy conversation and the apes can only speak in grunts and sounds as we formerly did? Is it possible that the apes are better off, or does man have the best of it? Undoubtedly speech, which also causes stress, is the basis of many mental break downs in the human species. Speaking has many faults. Perhaps the apes are living an easier life.

There doesn't seem to be any reason for either side having this difference, yet they do. Both seem to be satisfied, and I don't miss swinging through the trees. Both our body make-ups are similar, and there is no definite period of time wc can prove for which came into existence first, so I guess the best we can say about the whole thing is, "It's US and, We're having a ball!"

After all, we may look different to each other, but, as conglomerated matter in various sizes and shapes, we form each other. Total togetherness presents Mind/God.

Living is tough on your body. It is also tough on your pocket book and your mental stability! But damn, there's never been anything like or better than it.

We all came from the same friction, and we all, as a whole, contain the same plus or minus ingredients, elements, atoms, or quarks, or what ever it takes to form the matter we live in or with.

The environment is responsible for the physical and mental properties of Creation. The Mind is in command.

Pierre Teilhard de Chardin, in the closing words of his book, *Human Energy*, states, "In order to sustain and extend the huge, invincible and legitimate effort of research in which the vital weight of human activity is at present engaged, as faith, a mysticism is necessary."

Science, to me, has always expressed truth. The nearest I can come to resenting science is at a time of war, which seems to be always, scientists on both sides are being used to create methods of annihilation of the human race. Religions and political leaders blend together on opposite sides to settle their disputes over wealth and mysticism.

After thousands of years of relentless pursuit of a liberty which did or has never relied on their support, it was felt that the discovery of the true method by which life came about could never, or would never, be able to replace the heaven which was promised to them who led the perfect life. The various religions felt secure with their heaven, even though the Creation by God of the earth and its various forms were being threatened by this young science.

These men of science, although not agreeing on definite terms as to exactly how the progress of evolution works, still settled for the fact that evolution was and is a process of improvement. The study of fossilized bones of animals which no longer exist seems to be the beginning of the thought that something different than mythology has taken place. Naturally the various religions used these early discoveries as means of controlling their followers. The bones and shells are the result of a great flood that was brought about by God because the people of that time were not obeying his rules (made up by human beings), so this God killed them all (save but Noah and his family) by flooding the earth. Noah is supposedly the family we descended from.

Today, although nearly seven thousand years have passed, these same tales are being taught as truth to many both civilized and uncivilized nations in the same manner as they were in our past history. The same type leaders with the same warnings. However, there have been a few concessions on the part of the churches which have come about by being forced on the leaders by their followers. Scientists who have been educated in the church schools have advised the church to make many of these changes. Point in fact: Pope Paul's statement that the theory of evolution could now be taken as factual by the Roman Catholic Church.

In a recent issue of *Awake*, which is published semi-monthly by the Watchtower Bible and Tract Society of New York, as part of the Church for Jehovah's Witnesses, there was an article concerning the Universe which stated, "Did it come about by chance?" This article could really be part of what Haeckel referred to as the, "Dagger of Darkness." The article dealt with the galaxies for which Galileo had been imprisoned by the Inquisition in 1633 for advocating the sun was the center of our galaxy, rather than the earth. These same Inquisitions have closed the mouths of an astounding amount of church-educated scientists. Even Darwin had the feeling of being threatened if he exposed what he felt concerning the theory of evolution.

If all of our rules were changed overnight, and we were taught our true relationship, peace would come much sooner.

How long will it be before the leaders of Christianity and Islam will admit that Noah's Ark never existed?

Invention is likened to eating. It seems as though when a person has no hunger and is offered a bite of any sort of food, hunger takes over. An instance of an invention could be, in times past, the same thing. The art of throwing a rock by using a sling as leverage to toss it at higher speeds was the basis for the sling shot which David used to slay Goliath. The stone is simply put in a leather sling attached to one cord on each end and then twirled above the head. The faster the twirl, the faster the rock travels.

Our Creation of speech came after millions of years of physical evolution took place. There undoubtedly were many ideas that came to mind as we irked out different sounds, but again an absolute method of speech had to be developed along with the mouth, tongue and other parts. And then there was always the problem of coordination. Trial and error were used then, just as it is today. Perhaps the scream, as in most animals, came first, or it might have been our famous grunts. It's easy to understand the scream, even without context. A grunt could be taken in several ways, but mostly it was sort of like "okay".

The art of any of our inventions came about in a greater degree as we learned to sit and discuss in thoughts with others who had the same interest. I once wrote a few words about our ancestors sitting by a fire, and after several hours one of the "scientists" stood, and, with a long stick, scratched a line in the ground. Those watching grunted and murmured in astonishment. Moments later that "scientist" sat down, and another of the group stood and looked at the line. He took the stick from the other man, and, after studying for a few minutes, he placed the tip of the stick in the sand and drew a line that crossed the other line directly in the center to form an x. The murmuring and grunting were louder this time. The person gave the stick back to the original "scientist" and sat down. That was the lesson for the week.

Later there were others who added small extensions to this same x, and the design became a sign of good luck. It was several hundred thousands of years later when a madman took this same symbol and tried to conquer the world.

In *Man's Place in Nature*, Chardin continues to expose his thoughts concerning the mechanism of corpusulization, the transit to life. Difficult as this subject is, Chardin's explanation summed up the theory with, "There can be no doubt that this occurs." My ability to decipher his thought on two full pages fails to gather the gist of the meaning. However, his conclusion is easy to understand: "But for such a mechanism — we might call it 'unfettered moleculization' — to be initiated and to continue to operate, we must assume the existence and influence, underlying it, of some powerful dynamism."

That is the point to be stressed: an underlying dynamism: another exclamation for Mind/God.

The conclusion of Chardin expresses in the background of the subject of his explanation of the beginning of life lies, or stands, or exists a powerful dynamism that is responsible for the mechanism which is directing the Creation and actions of man. Could it not be possible that this powerful dynamism is truly exhibiting itself through humankind and the rest of Creation? Mankind, although only being a part of existence, seems to be enjoying their position as leaders here on earth. By this I mean all Creation makes up what Chardin refers to as the powerful dynamism. There is no powerful dynamism working in the background. This powerful dynamism could also be what causes a young bird to peck its way out of the shell, or the baby kangaroo to climb to its mother's pouch with its eyes still sealed. This Powerful Dynamism is living its existence through universal Creation. This same Powerful Dynamism exists everywhere throughout the universe, and it is Its desire to exist in the best and easiest manner possible. Although It exists in the animate as well as the inanimate, It too exists in the Seen as well as the Unseen. Everything must exist through what brings about existence. Mankind, a partial source of the method of existence for the Powerful Dynamism, has come to be through Its efforts to Be and wears the uniform of Creation. Some feel not to be a part of this Creation, while others relish in this gift of life. To Be part of Creation offers each the opportunity to express themselves in a manner which exposes easier methods for existence. This existence, which entombs all Creation, is a continuous desire by Creation throughout the universe to exist in the same surroundings. And exist we will. The sum total for this reasoning is that there is no desire for nonexistence.

Recently, possibly three years ago, I wrote about speaking in the present tense. When a person says, "So and so was so nice, she used to tell me funny stories," it puts them in a past tense. If a person would say, "So and so is so nice, she always tells me funny stories," it puts them in present tense. Present tense presents life. It's much better in the present tense.

Mind, being you and everything else, puts a person in the same position. If you put yourself in the position of being the Mind as a whole and existing through the Universal Creation, eternity is yours.

In biology and sociology the basic meaning of the word evolution is transformation to higher levels of complexity. If this is true, does the basic single cell transform to the higher level multicell, or does the single cell remain as the multicell is developed? In my opinion, evolution continues to develop higher and higher complexities, while those it evolved through continue to be as they are, and partial extinction occurs when the vitality of another organ is no longer needed or able to exist.

Creation is most often mentally looked at as a happening of the past. Creation as a fact is in control of eternity. At this time it appears that there is no possible means of destroying Creation. Creation is matter in all forms. Matter is CONTINUAL. It cannot be destroyed. True, it can be dissolved in various manners. However, dissolution in any way merely presents matter as another solution. Transformation of matter may be achieved through heat, cold, or subtraction or addition of atoms to its structure. Creation reacts through evolution for the survival of itself, which describes the finite to the infinite. Creation might be thought of as the Great Controller. After all, Creation is Mind/God's manner of exposing Itself to Itself. If this were not true, how would life know how to express the correct manner in which to exist?

I feel a desire expounds its energy through Creation while aspiring to promote an existence in the easiest possible way. No tricks are played; nothing has preference over anything else. The value of vitality is not wealth, rather self-satisfaction in exercising good judgment: the object of life.

Brain is Brain. Not hers, yours, his or mine. It's not theirs or any other of Creation's. Brain is matter and designed to contain, or converse, with Mind. Mind, a metamorphous of spirit, serves as the directional part of a force we'll describe as freedom. Freedom, in our case, could mean security. Security is our attachment to eternity. Everything has this, we just haven't realized we couldn't exist without it. Our force of Being has passed through a procession of Being, for what you might consider as billions of years.

What Brain consists of is pure matter, just as all of the soles or bodies of all Creation. These soles or bodies house Brain, and Mind comes and goes. Mind is the direct connection to what we refer to as God. Mind receives its basic instructions from the force of desire and is the primary drive of reaction from what we have learned to refer to as God.

It is so plain to see, and almost everyone who gets to ride in an automobile and is lucky enough to head out of town and along the country roads and have seen mountains and canyons where it is possible to count the layers of earth that are exposing themselves, that these giant plates have broken apart and their force has caused them to over-ride one another. Some of the smaller pieces, or plates, are even up-ended. And there are those that have sunk into the magma and disappeared. Dissolution perhaps is the solution to Atlantis. There may never have been an Atlantis, but I'd bet a two dollar bill there has been more than one tribal nation that has disappeared in this same way.

More than we have reckoned for could happen again. The Hawaiian Islands are a good example, and it's still happening there.

I forgot to mention, as you already know, it has taken a few billion years.

At times I feel that humankind has spent so much time convincing itself of its self-importance by comparing itself to the rest of Creation, that it may be impossible to estrange themselves from the idea of superiority before the annihilation of planet earth takes place. Perhaps it will serve us right. Then we'll all suffer together.

In his book, *The Big Bang Never Happened*, Eric Lerner wrote, "As I write this, I happen to be in an airplane at 30,000 feet, flying over Wyoming en route home from San Francisco to Boston. Below, the earth looks very soft and comfortable- fluffy clouds here and there, snow turning pink as the sun sets, road stretching———."

The mention of pink snow by Lerner perked my senses. The first time I ever tasted pink snow was also in the state of Wyoming. I was up in the Great Beartooth Wilderness Area in northeastern Wyoming, right next to Yellowstone National Park. I was guiding some fisherman to the high lakes in the area after golden trout. We were about ten-thousand feet above sea level. This was in the late seventies. I had seen pink clouds before, and also small pink specs in these same high lakes, but had never paid much attention to them. I have watched many times as the fish swim in the shallow water purposely stirring up the silt in the shallow water making the tiny pink specks drift to the surface. On their return, the fish swam through the pink specks with their mouths open eating them.

A friend told me they were shrimp, but I could see no comparison. The pink specs in the snow seem to come from the atmosphere. When a person smells and tastes a handful of this pink snow, it tastes and smells just like watermelon. Besides this, when you clean and smell both the grayling and white fish of this high terrain country, both smell and taste like watermelon. I've often wondered if these same pink dots don't condense in the clouds and drop to the earth from the atmosphere.

Besides pink snow, grayling, and whitefish, these are the only three things I've ever tasted and smelled that had the same taste and odor of watermelon.

Herbert Spencer and Henri Bergson both mentioned this same pink snow in their writings of the 1850s.

They say that the alligator is one of the oldest living animals on the planet earth that has remained in almost the same shape that it acquired many millions of years ago in our past, prehistoric history. Naturally it did not begin as an alligator and had to pass through the flames of beginning with us. However, once it had acquired, in early prehistory, its present physical appearance, it became satisfied with what it had to work with, and there seemed to be no need for further rise or development for it to survive in a very relaxed physical and mental condition. The way it now appears, extreme heat or cold could be its only harm, excepting humankind in late centuries who seem to have created a great desire for alligator shoes and purses. In any event, there seems to be no desire on behalf of this indestructible beast to improve on its physical or mental being. It has succeeded in proving its ability both to protect itself and acquire food in a very admirable way; in natural disasters or emergencies the alligator seems to be able to survive in a sort of hibernation stage. Total satisfaction seems to have replaced desire and the urge for further evolutionary development.

There are many others who have not been as lucky as the alligator. There seems to be nothing in our modern time that resembles the brachiosaurs, a member of the dinosaur family who has become extinct except for their pedal extremes. The feet of this largest of all animals seem to have been carried forth in the elephant and the rhinoceros.

Even the body of the most terrible of all, Tyrannosaurs Rex, resembles that of a chicken. There are many comparable parts of all animals that plainly display or exhibit themselves in their kin of this, our twenty-first century. And undoubtedly there will be many more in our future. The birds we call pigeons have so many different forms and abilities they strain our imagination. When I was a young man, I crossed a tumbler with a roller and raised young birds which I could not turn loose. The reason was when they flew and attempted to tumble they never stopped tumbling and fell to the ground smashing their small bodies. Charles Darwin used pigeons as one of his main subjects in his "theoretical" studies of the principle of evolution. Just minutes ago my friend Bennii was using raid to exterminate some flies in the bathroom. She called me to come and see two flies that were evidently breeding when they were sprayed. I went to see, and there they were evidently held together by their sex organs just like a pair of dogs butt to butt. That's a new one. I had never seen anything but dogs stuck together in this same fashion in all my 76 years.

Hermes Trismegistus in his writings, *The Divine Pymander*, which was approximated as being written before ancient Grecian times, explained that before any of humankind can see or be near God, they must break through the garment, or sole, which they wear and covers the flesh and body of their Being. In other words, escape from the interference of their outside appearance and its control of the mental stabilities of their bodies.

It seems odd that a God, after spending millions and millions of years in evolutionizing a body as good and adept as what we, as a part of Creation, now have, would tell us to tear it to pieces and escape from its control. This control, Hermes tell us, is leading us astray and is concluded as being sinful.

I'm sure old Trigger was on the wrong path. After all, sin is Life. We are born out of sin, as some religious leaders tell us.

I'm sure there are many of us now who would thank Hermes for the efforts he put forth in his writings, trying to help when civilization was getting started.

Happiness cannot be contained forever. When unhappiness occurs, one must take advantage of it. In this manner happiness becomes greater.

They tell us that man is born through an act of sin. If this is true, then why didn't our Great Conceiver make the achievement of generation an effort rather than one of our greatest pleasures?

Could the reason be that if generation were and effort instead of pleasure, generation would concede to failure? Life's struggle would be greatly increased.

Hermes Mercurius Trismegistus says that God is in the Mind, the Mind in the Soul, the Soul in the Matter, all things by Eternity.

The results are God is Mind, Mind influences Matter, Matter fills Organs. Organs are vessels in which matter exists.

Eternity is achieved through the evolution of organs. The results of this force are absorbed and digested by Mind and presented on the table of Life from which All may choose.

Hermes Mercurius Trismegistis spoke to Tat, his son, "Seeing then the world is all formed, what must He Be that made it? For without form He cannot Be." Hermes continued, "If therefore thou wilt not equal thyself to God, thou cannot understand God: for the Like is intelligible by the Like."

If Like is intelligible to Like, as Hermes explains, then Like must furnish Like to All Beings. For God to be only like man would mean God is only God to man.

"If therefore thou wilt not equal thyself to All Beings, thou canst visualize God as God to All."

Therefore if this thought does not adjust your thought, then there must be a God for each different Being.

This would present the physical aspects of a product of the evolutionary process.

At all times I must praise the God that created me, together with all Creation. For this God is all things that Creation and I are, this God is All things we do; this God is all things we say; this God is all things we think.

This God lives within all Creation and me. No matter how many times we pass through the process of birth, this God lives within All Creation no matter what type sole we wear; this God lives within Me through all righteousness; this God provides Creation and Me with Life in all forms; this God provides the universal atmosphere for all Creation and me to continue to breath Life; this God generates into the lungs of all that Be. Existence is God: God is existence Eternal.

The spirit labors through grief. The Spirit perks through the actions of happiness. The Spirit rests through the attachment of love. The spirit is steadfast through the actions of wrath. The Spirit displays compassion during the period of forgiveness.

In his tenth book, *The Mind Of Hermes*, Trismegistis wrote, "...for they are Bodies, and have a Soul, and are moved."

As it should have been written, "for they are organs, and have Spirit which moves them."

"Matter and Soul, " as Hermes scrolls, seem drab. Matter and Spirit seem a much better unification.

Life is the only circumstance that has no antithesis. Even the All-seeing eye encompasses Life. Life Itself sees Life. Perhaps if Life Itself were not, what would take Life's place? As Bergson writes: there can be no *nothing*; the void cannot exist.

God has forever, perhaps, been referred to as He or Him. Gender towards God can only be exhibited through the animation of the animated Creation. Respect of the female is continually exposed in their actions. God to be included in the makeup of Creation must be included in all matter. This we are taught, "God lives in everything," or, "God is everything."

This would make those of us feel as though God were a sightless vapor filling the atmosphere and all other matter. God is Eternity, Eternally. One of Eternity's meanings in Webster's is, "The endless time after death." Death is explained in the same book as, "The act or fact of dying, permanent ending of all life in a person, animal, or plant."

It's easy to accept the explanation of Eternity in the Webster's Dictionary, but to throw God out the window with that explanation of death is hard to accept. If one thing must die, then all things must die. Even though God would be left as only an Atmosphere of Being, whoever would know He, She, or It would still be alive. For fact, how would God know It was still alive if there were none to explain the situation?

Trismegistis spoke as He, God, informed him, "For there is One Soul, One Life, and One God." In the 1950's, I wrote over and over, "One God-One Soul." My reason, perhaps, was I never took into Mind the true explanation of the word soul. It was not until 1980 that I commenced seeing the difference.

Spirit is the effervescence that secures life, which is breath and vitality. All Life contains Spirit: the Soul, as we are taught, only belongs to humankind. I cannot envision a Heaven with only Humankind, even if the streets are paved with gold. Neither can God!

Now poets can speak as they feel. In past history, it cost them their lives. That went with the game.

Today I'm better off than ever. I've spent millions and millions of years, and more, to achieve life as it is today. I live as the cosmos, the atmosphere, the elements, and all sorts of matter. My mind is in the organs of all Creation, my feelings are the feelings of all, my thoughts are the thoughts of all. Today I make sounds through the animated and speak through the tongue of humankind. Speech has become common to all humankind, Voice is proper to all living.

Now, together, we almost have the understanding of what we feel to be understanding. Peace is in sight of our Being. There now are those who stand side by side and watch as others are led astray. Help has at last entered the scene. No longer are all against all, and no longer will the stranger convince the stranger to go to war.

At last we can stand together with all Creation and enjoy the benefits of what we have all learned together. I, as all, have been forced to live and struggle. Just as Creation has searched me out, I have had to search Creation out. I, too, have wondered about life. I, too, have passed through the stress of desire.

Today I am as you, and all Creation, just as it has always been. The difference being together our mind and spirit see one another; all of this has brought about satisfaction of understanding that we are All together as One; and We're having a ball!

Where the organ is thickest, the senses are weakest!

Fate or faith — which is it? Fate can be awarded the individual from both sides. Faith is rewarded the individual from the side they chose.

From the basic being, Mind, Hermes Trismegistis concludes that, "...the animated all contain Mind, however, in humankind, the Mind is more than the rest of the animated." As it appears to the desires of Mind itself, Mind is sized to fit all. Even those who are inanimate contain Mind, as well as the rest of Creation. Meekness merely requires less.

"Necessity, providence and nature are the organs of instruments of the world and the order of matter," writes Hermes Trismegistis. "For of those things that are intelligence, everyone is; but the Essence of them is identity. For the bodies that are put together, and that have, and make their changes in to other, having this identity, do always save and preserve the incorruption of the identity.

But in every one of the compound or human bodies there is a number.

For without number it is impossible there should be consistence or constitution, or composition, or dissolution.

But Unities do both beget and increase Numbers, and again being dissolved, come into themselves.

And the matter is one."

The results of these thoughts could have been the birth of the *Book of Numbers* in the Old Testament. Remember, "Come and be numbered, or the gates of heaven will be closed to you."

I'm going to mix my thoughts with Hermes' thoughts. Hermes, while talking to his son Tat, says, "Know generally, O Son, that whatsoever is in the World, is moved either according to Augmentation or Diminution." In simple language, either becoming or fading, which is a truth of life to all.

"Yet, Tat, nothing is corrupted or destroyed. Generation is not life, but sense; neither is change death, but forgetfulness, or rather Occultation, and lying hid."

Hermes came very close to the true answer to the question of eternity. He used, "lying hid" to explain a connection to eternity.

"Or better this," Hermes added, "for generation is not a Creation of life, but a production of things to sense, and making them manifest. Neither is change death, but an Occultation or a hiding of that which was."

From the results of Generation a production is assembled. This production, if everything goes well, due to the chromosomes of both parents and ancestors, will resemble them all.

Augmentation immediately takes place. Every instant of life, from birth, is seen by those who come in contact or watch this Being as it proceeds through life. The actions are carefully analyzed and digested. Looks and movements are digested by others. This same holds true by the production itself. Looks, movements, speech, etc., are all judged by others and stockpiled in Mind for future use. That is if others decide they like what the production shows. In other words, mimicking, or copying of the good things, used by others. Good things might be bad things to some, but to the bad they, too, are good.

The properties of the production are passed on to become a living part of Creation. In early history, mankind absorbed the actions of all animated Creation and learned to create nests, then huts, and then houses. Or gliders and then airplanes by watching the birds. Or from beavers they learned to build dams. Everything seen went into the bank we call Mind for future use.

Upon the completion of Augmentation, Diminution commences, and the same actions take place between the production and the rest of Creation until the time of dissolution.

With dissolution the process of generation begins. At this time a vessel, or organ of a different design may be used, but the same Spirit and Mind are there, as God, and all of the billions times billions of actions and appearances are drawn from the senses to create another who will have the advantage of past looks and experiences.

Generation after generation after generation are a continuation of this same process of evolution. Eternity is stronger in each generation due to the improvements learned. The masses and matter act as a bank. The Mind and Spirit are God. The production comes in the organ or body of any part of Creation and lives through the Mind and Spirit as a part of what we now refer to as God. Eternity as always is the result of production. Production is Creation; Creation is God; God is Eternal to physical and mental evolution.

The *Dawn Of Satisfaction* presents the abolishment of mental mythology.

It took me nearly fifty years to replace the god I had before — the one who made people out of mud.

Dissolution: to breakup, dissolve. Dissolve: to loosen asunder, disunite. Transitive senses. To reduce to its formative elements, to cast aside the physical integrity. To disintegrate or decompose through fire or rot. To release something from Being. But not death, for death is merely dissolution, and nothing has ever been put to death. The organs which carry the flesh and sap, of what so far has only been a manufactured necessity, will continue in change.

The physical has surrendered to that which comes after, and yet that, together with what the organ contained, have scarred the sign of progress for the better. No nitch can pass unnoticed. This is eternity.

The Spirit must be a part of each organ or vessel. No matter the size. My ability to say this is allowed through the fact that it is possible for any of Creation to raise or lower his or her own Spirit. True, it can be effected by other Beings. However, the Spirit belongs to the particular organ or vessel in which it thrives through Brain, which is an organ that is a physical relative to the Aetheristic Spirit.

The difference between Spirit and Mind are that Creation receives through Mind. When the organ begins the process of dissolution and becomes feeble, Brain is passing along the same pathway. Mind is as strong as ever; It's the receiver that is fading, along with the rest of the flesh and organs. It is the organ or vessel that contain Brain, the bed of Mind, that face the obligation of dissolution. It is through the organ or vessel of all Creation that Mind momentarily losses connection with true life, as life takes an instant to generate.

Lies are playthings. Truth is life.

Scientists throughout the world seem to have accepted evolutionary progress in both the physical and mental make-up of the Universal Creation as fact today. However, there seems to still be the question of how does the mechanics of evolution come about or, in plain words, work? The thought of it happening far outdates any actual study. Just as many creatures of Creation are still passing through the process of evolutionary development, there stands no proof of the method by which it works.

If immortality of the individual is true, evolution is not possible. Any form of evolution can only be true with the unfolding of matter to a different form. Being it ever so slight and ever so slow. Matter can only be evolved through dissolution- augmentation, dissolution-augmentation, etc.

All life is created by the desire or power to Be and contained in the organ. This includes all, or any part of, Creation. Each part has its organ within the organ of another. The Maker or Originator can also be found AS the organ of All..

Is it possible that humankind migrated from the water on two legs? A fact is that we passed continuously through evolution from the single cell as all Creation. Our size, just as the prehistoric reptiles, was regulated according to our fuel supply. We still have midgets here on earth. Perhaps the midgets, in pre-history, gave birth to even smaller midgets. Midgets had midgets, etc, etc. It is very easy to believe we might have once been the size of a mite, with just as many colors. After all we're related to All — every "body" knows that, and what difference does it make concerning our size or how long it took?

Unless stabilized, any object thrown into the atmosphere will spin. The higher the speed, the faster the spin, providing the weight is the same, just as the size.

The higher the speed, in the same atmospheric pressure, the warmer the object becomes. This continues to the melting point, and fumes of the atmosphere fractionalize flame. The magnetic force of the sun holds the earth at bay with this same gravitational force, pulling the earth on track as it spins around and around a flaming ball of life we call sun, "Good morning America."

If two droplets of water are placed side by side and suddenly, without notice or infringement, they become one, then Satisfaction is the result.

If there is such a thing as soul, does death place it? Or send it? Or is it left up to the shaman, like we "thought" it used to be?

Hominid: any of a family of two-legged primates including all forms of humans, extinct and living. Could this include extinct species of the human race that possibly walked on four legs or swam the seas?

Hominy: parched corn with the germ removed. A meal created by boiling the corn.

There must be a relationship between the two words, hominid, and hominy. My suggestion might be both include many kernels or seeds.

Chardin speaks of the World evolving towards the spirit. Spirit is not a whole that reacts spontaneously through the reactions of the multitudes, unless the multitudes are gathered together witnessing the home team or other events that favor the local citizenship. Spirit itself is the property of each individual and is under the control of each being to have a low spirit or a high spirit. It makes no difference in the type body or organ the individual wears. High and low spirits affect all forms of life. Spiritual affect comes closest to the true sense of feeling. To say one feels bad presents low spirits. The opposite of this is to feel good and automatically raise the spirits. To be in high spirits is very good. If a person is in high spirits, and he visits a person in low spirits, only an attempt can be made to raise the low spirits of the other. Spirit does not come to two individuals under the same circumstances. Spirit belongs to all. Up or down is entirely a personal feeling. To change the mode of a spirit is up to the individual. Attempts can be made by others to help, and sometimes they do. However, the individual creature must be the one that raises or lowers their own spirit. As a whole, spirit is in the pleasant mode for all. To have the spirit raised is on an equal basis with having the spirits lowered.

Spirits are raised and lowered by Mind. Spirit itself cannot affect itself. Spirit in reality is only a word for feeling. Spirit has no power on its own. Spirit can only react as the organ feels.

If you see someone who has been frost bitten from severe cold, such as forty below zero F^0, the frost bitten areas on their body appear to have been caused by scalding hot water or flames, rather than severe cold. This would prove that heat and cold cause the same reaction of disintegration. Either one breaks matter down, which in reality is only change. Torrid flames, torrential rain, and unending lightning caused thunder to roll over a frothing sphere we now call earth.

What might be called the beginning of our planet was really life becoming on a new home for Creation.

"Motivations do not only acute or operate living and breathing, Bodies, they also cause Bodies of Wood, Stones, and such to increase and bear fruit, or ripen. Corrupting, rotting, putrefying, and breaking, are also a motivation, and bring about what so ever all inanimate Bodies can suffer." These are the words of Hermes Trismegistis in his book *Of Operation and Sense*, and are used by Hermes to disclose his conception of a Soul which belongs only to humankind.

In his book within a book, *The Key*, Hermes tells us that, "...for the soul without Mind, can neither do, nor say anything; for many times the Mind flies away from the Soul, and in that hour the Soul neither seeth nor heareth, but is like an unreasonable thing; so great is the power of the Mind."

Searching out the Soul and its proper place in Creation places many obstacles on the pathway. However, I cannot release from my mind its original explanation. The noun "sole," in its original use, was to refer to the physical appearance of any of Creation, this was long before religion or any part of it had invented heaven. Some method had to be conceived as a manner in which to let another know they were referring to the outside appearance of the organ in which the matter and other organs live. Sole, I believe, was the word first used by Creation for all shapes or forms.

I have spent most of my lifetime on the planet earth in an effort to free humankind, and the rest of Creation, from the grips of organized religion.

Since the conception of life, the various religions have forced their ways on humankind, forever excusing themselves for the actions in the past which wasted the energy of Being many times over.

The possibility of our life extending into the future through the process of evolution, to me, has now become a fact. It has made it impossible for me to retire and feel that whatever will be will be. I must continue due to the circumstances that I now understand. Mine and your security in the future relies on how we handle our bound duties concerning life as it is today.

It is getting better. Perhaps, in the future, life will become as good as It can get!

There are many who could have told us more. There are many reasons for their not doing so. However, their main reason to search no more was their fear of a God they were taught to fear.

There are more exertion forces at the north and south poles of our planetary sphere than at its equator. True, the equator travels fastest due to circumference, but the poles are digesting both the positive and negative molecules of atmospheric indulgence.

The God of the evolutionist is Creation!
God to the evolutionist is Creation!
The evolutionist must worship Creation!
There's nothing else, Creation must be God!
Why would someone create Creation? To be alone?
It appears that God had been unable to expose
Itself, for the past billions of years, in
any other way than Creation.

The thoughts of man must ebb just as the tides of the seas. It is during this mental ebb tide that the Mind receives the power to create. The lower the ebb, the stronger the thought.

Mind has been directly connected to the power to Be since Creation was conceived. The desire to Be has been achieved since conceivement, through Mind.

From nonexistence to existence proves the fact of an un-fore-seen Mind that has steadily evolved the body of Creation, and today thrives as Itself throughout the Universal Atmosphere. Name it as you please — it is there.

As this process unfolds, the desire to Be has had to wrap Itself in the thought of what is to be created. This thought, although pure etheric in the beginning, just as it happens in the mental make-up of Mind in all Creation today, is forced to mentally create a solution to Being.

Mind must create a place of dwelling in which It, the unseen, can dwell and create another Being, even more than It's original Creation. Life through this Creation Is.

Mind now has many physical animated vessels or organs in which to Be and Be physically seen, no matter Its size.

Existence must be furnished through thought, as a Being, before Creation becomes. Just as Jesus fed the multitudes' thought for existence, Existence must feed Its cells with thought. Zillions of these cells come into existence throughout the cosmic universe daily and will continue to be produced throughout eternity. Mind will guide them, while existing in them.

After all of the different studies concerning Mind or Spirit, in which we trust as the most sincere and which is always there in a pinch, the Mind is presented. Mind seems to be our direct connection to things we, or a part of us, call God. There are many other words in many languages which use different pronunciations or words to describe this Identical God I am speaking of. However, in my case, Mind is best.

All creatures, both seen and unseen, contain Brain. Brain is the reflection of Mind.

Mind controls all vital activities of all creatures through Brain.

Mind makes Itself available to all matter through Brain.

Through Brain, the Mind digests and processes life.

Mind is each organ's connection to eternity.

Nothing has, or will, exist beyond the apprehension of Mind, including Desire.

Mind generates Being. Being expresses life.

Life lives through Mind eternally.

The evolutionary process of our bodies makes life easier for Mind. This is compensation for the effort of Being.

Just because our existence seems to average around seventy-years is no reason we should regret spending this lifetime on planet earth.

There's quite a span between seventy-years and fifteen-billion years, the time earth has been here. We scream out we want a fair deal for our seventy-years of existence. What's in it for us and our time on this planet, and what do we think our time is worth?

There's got to be more to It than this life. Mind continually helps us to understand!

Scientists toy today with the ancient vessels which make up the matter that had satisfied our needs to exist as organs billions of years ago. Any shape, any size, any matter, our needs require energy. Things require the existence of lots of other things in order to survive themselves.

Life has always exploded with ideas for existence. It had to; it is the only means of survival. Life and evolution present Eternity.

There are hundreds of languages that are read or spoken throughout our planet earth. Yet Mind converses to all from this same intelligence.

I've tried in many ways to convince others of this same intelligence contained in all forms of life, from the measureless to the immeasurable. Perhaps it might be thought that comprehension or awareness could possibly be the very beginning we all speak of.

What construes as Brain seems to be fathomless. Medulla is at the head of the spinal or nerve chord and seems to be the first recognized part of Brain. However, there are millions of things smaller that contain Brain. When you are smaller than a cell, there must still be Brain.

In his book *Cosmos*, Carl Sagan wrote, "If we plunged through a pore into the nucleus of the cell, we would find something that resembles an explosion in a spaghetti factory — a disorderly multitude of coils and strands, which are the two kinds of nucleic acids: DNA, which knows what to do, and RNA, which conveys the instructions issued by DNA to the rest of the cells. These are the best that four billion years of evolution could produce, containing cell, a tree, or a human work. The amount of information in human DNA, if written out in ordinary language, would occupy a hundred thick volumes. What is more, the DNA molecules know how to make, with only very rare exceptions, identical copies of themselves. They know extraordinarily much."

It's a shame that a person like Sagan, who devoted almost his entire life to science, has to listen to others quarrel about other animals, besides humans, having an inferior Brain. After all it takes Brain to prove what DNA and RNA understand.

To continue one's duties for existence, one must realize what they are, and what is the reward that produces their attachment to eternity. Admitting to yourself and to other parts of Creation that Mind speaks through matter is to understand that Matter cannot be destroyed. Matter is existence; your reward for Being is expressed in the eternity of matter, with Mind being the director through DNA and good old-fashioned medulla. They've both been around forever. Soon we'll add another name of something that's been here longer than both DNA and medulla.

A certainty is what we all search for to give ourselves a foundation of Being.

Certain things are certain. One of these things is Mind we possess which we share with the Master of Creativity. Mind is also shared with every Being of friction or matter as a part of Creation. It is an equal connection of One to All and All to One. It is impossible to teach that Mind only belongs to certain objects of Creation who have been lucky enough to be "chosen," and also a thing that came as a direct gift from some god.

The reason Mind must be shared by all is that pure evolution has presented a continual change in the physical appearance of all matter. Since the dawn of Creation, change has continued to unfold. Mind is our activation as friction for the single cell just as it is for our planetary system. Time, as we know it, may or may not be of importance, and is used mostly as comparison. However, humankind seem to have been taught that time brings about age; age brings about decay; decay, most have been educated to believe, results in transformation and is a result of death; transformation might be considered to be neutralization.

Time is just a word. The progress of birth is the design and construction of serviceable requirements. These two are the basic requirements for pure mental and physical evolution. The progress of this developmental process allows all of us to fit in with the locomotion and the momentum of progress. As a necessity, pure evolution many times has to succumb to the wraths of progress. Formation of our planet earth is a perfect example. Vast catastrophes have presented themselves while our process to Be has silently evolutionized to Become as we are. These instances of vast desolation have happened in many ways. However, I can imagine the worse to take place is when the plates, which make up the crust, are forced to give way to one another as the earth cools and shrinks, causing them to override one another. As most of the scientific world is aware, change of diet is the easiest way to bring physical evolution into action. It's plain to see that when the plates shifted, there had to be great changes in the natural environment.

When someone tells or writes that man, as humanity, is a recent development, of say the last twenty million years, it could possibly be truth, considering the physical appearance of humankind as they are today. To be able to reverse our thought and pass back beyond this imagination, we must put the physical shape of man in a different prospective. We must remove one of our prize possessions, the opposable thumb, and replace it with, let's say, a set of claws like the crabs have. Let's put the eyes of humanity on stems so we can see all around ourselves. Or maybe a fish while water was our environment. It is factual truth mankind did not always promenade throughout the countryside in lush meadows as they do today, dressed in shorts and wearing Nike shoes. Besides all of this, it is our greatest need to always keep in Mind that we also exist with what we see in nature. Humanity does not exist separately. If we did, we would have no relationship to one another. The mode of existence is our bond to Life.

Now the blow comes. While you are seeing yourself as I have tried to convince you, you must realize that Mind we have is Mind of all. We, and our partners, including all organs of Creation, are the masters of life. We make up the thing we call, or refer to as the Master of Creation. We, through Mind, are the Creator. Along with all of the rest of Creation, either microscopic or macroscopic, all Beings in all types of vessels conglomerated in all types of matter together, through Mind, make up the Master. Our total Creation survives through Life. It will be impossible in the future for any of Creation to survive the natural impositions in the vessel or body in the exact same shape and condition, inside and out, that We are wearing today. Just as twenty-million years ago we had to appear in a vessel a great deal different than it is today.

"If this is so, then what's in it for me?" That's the question in the MIND of all. People should ask, "What's in it for us?" meaning ALL Creation. The answer then would be much simpler.

If we ALL exist through our appearance or affect, then we ALL must be related. "How are we related?" In our mental and physical make-up! Each shares Mind, which proves the value of consciousness to each of it users. The users are manufactured into life in billions and billions of physical shapes. Very few of these can be seen with the human eye but are sensed by one another. The same thing is true for the planets, the masters of the Universe. "What's in it for Us?"

is the same thing for all forever. The unfolding of physical progress has presented us the appliances of pleasure. We live in an almost Shangri-la as far as conveniences are concerned. Our automotion could be considered almost the best yet, other than de-gravitating ourselves. True, our pets and other parts of Creation can only share in these through their share of mental being. If it is good for others, it is good for us — all life belongs to all Life.

What about decay? Death. Death is both disintegration and an instance of birth. Or possibly we could refer to it as an instant of configuration. First, the mental progress of Mind relies on the suggestions received through our mental kinship or relationship. Everything that has ever taken place is in the Mind through the process of Mental Evolution. Nothing can nor will ever be left out. It must be digested into the governing body of pure evolution that is Creation. To toss things to the wind — or consider anything useless — is not a part of life. Each of All life, to Be, requires the existence of all Life.

"It seems to me this has happened before!" Probably not only once, but billions of times to all Creation; this is what presents pure, undisturbed evolution.

From the micro-happenings of our personal existence to the macro-happening of the atomic bombs released over Japan, all enter the hall of records of evolution. This is eternity, and you cannot escape being there! It's impossible for anything to exist without contributing to the universe of Being.

There is no possible way to stop the evolutionary progress of matter towards a more peaceful way of existence through comparison by Mind.

Life required someone, or something, to take the first chance.

Spirit, no matter it's status, is eternal.

Eternity is received through eternal transcendence — eternally transpiring while eternally transforming.

What Jesus said in a simple sentence, it takes priests and politicians an entire sermon to relate.

Love is the communion of spirit with spirit.

Those who made up the miracles and stunts that Jesus is said to have performed, and then expounded them, are causing Jesus to suffer today. "The truth shall set you free."

The will to Be exposes Itself just as shredded flesh conglomerates to heal itself.

When any of Creation moves towards a waterhole, this is the desire to Be, no matter the consequences.

With all of the misery of backaches confronting the human race, perhaps we arose from walking on four legs too soon.

Be patient!

Just because we're made of matter doesn't prove we really need it.

Through the exposure of our past by scientific research, it is easy now to look back and see how the different religions have conceded to science concerning the growth of our natural world-planet-earth for the benefit of their followers — who would no longer be listening if the religions had not made concessions.

Mind is the true conceiver of life. When an attempt is completed to get to the core of life, in future thought, it will be proven that Mind assembled life through thought.

The weight of life does not effect the newborn. This for-ever process allows imagination to develop.

It all started when I was re-examining the definition of the word protozoa in the *Oxford Dictionary*. Protozoa is explained as, "...one of the two (or three) great divisions of the animal kingdom, comprising animals of the simplest or most primitive type, each consisting of a single cell, usually of microscopic size." Proto, a Greek word in the Oxford Dictionary, comprises four pages, approximately two thousand words which explains it as being before the nouns listed. The noun in the base of protozoa, is zoa. Zoa's definition is plural for zoon. Zoon, as described by Herbert Spencer in the same dictionary, means, "An organism scientifically regarded as complete animal, i.e. one which is the total product of an impregnated ovum, whether constituting a single being as in the higher animals, or a number of distinct beings (zooids) as in the successive asexual generation of aphides or the various 'persons' that make up a compound or colonial animal."

So protozoa is an animal in the animal kingdom which is microscopically small. So small that sometimes it can only be thought of through the mind's mechanisms.

Samuel Coleridge (1772-1834), a poet and outstanding scientific writer and philosopher, stated in 1834 that, "The lowest class of animals, or protozoa, have neither Brain nor nerves." This statement is just the opposite of my personal feelings, and yet the article in Encyclopedia Britannica goes on to say that Coleridge was a very staunch member of society at that time referred to as the pantisocratic scheme, a scheme designed to build a better society. A pantisocratic is being a person who advocates or promotes pantisocracy, pantisocrat being one involved in a social organization in which all are equal in rank and social position; a Utopian community in which all are equal and all rule.

Physical evolution at this time was almost a hidden science. This could possibly be the reason for Coleridge feeling the protozoan had no Brain or nervous system. Although he advocated the equal relationship of all larger animals of the animal kingdom, he felt it was impossible for something so small you cannot see to contain Brain. Through Brain ALL Creation exists and live as equals.

To have Being, Mind must demonstrate Itself through ALL Creation.

Mind: the seat of a person's consciousness, thoughts, volitions, and feelings.

Mind: the system, or process of knowing including both awareness and judgment.

Mind: the controller of the actions of flora and fauna (matter).

Mind's Eye: the mental act of conceiving physically.

Mind: the element or complexity of elements in any Being that feels, perceives, thinks, wills or reasons.

Mind: the master of intention or Desire.

Mind: in Christian Science, God.

Can it be that Mind Telesme evolutionary processes produce the Universe through desire?

Conclusions expose Creation as Mercury relates to transformation!

I feel in my heart there is more life in the atmospheric frictions and vapors than upon all the planets combined. After all, these are what the universe is made of.

The Mind is naught but thought. Yet all things are created through Mind's desire.

The energy of Mind conceives through friction, a force unseen. Yet from Mind the Universe became

Nothing can be taken from something that has been created from void. The wind blows from nowhere and yet goes nowhere. It has no destination and came from there.

The Mind constructs Creation, and Creation devours Creation. Existence is the pay off.

The time is drawing eternally closer when Creation will be affected by the words which have been expressed as the philosophy of calmness or composure. A right, or the right to think and to express oneself, shall belong to all!

No political power shall exist until one is developed which displays that which the society enforces, and is truly a branch of our ultimate goal: egalitarianism.

Just as the progress of physical evolution has forced Creation to physical achievements, mental evolution will force the natural sciences, through its general laws, to present Creation as an understanding of its Being. As Condorcet asked in 1795, "Why should this evolutionary principal be any less true for the development of the intellectual and moral facilities than for other physical operations of nature?"

This is Condorcet's sketch for *A Historical Picture of The Progress of the Human Mind.*

Pascal had compared the human race to a man who never dies. Which It is — continually gaining knowledge.

Total Mind retains a reflective life through Brain, physically and mentally forcing its persistence of intelligence in the direction of the comprehension as the true meaning of life, which in total equals the sum of positive and negative. It is up to the Mind, as a part of your brain, to guide the energy received. When positive and negative make contact and supply energy, you must personally direct this energy towards what you feel would furnish the best, or most, for Creation, which is also the best way for you!

Evolution is the science of natural relationship!

Mind created Brain to expose Itself through, not to create mythological views concerning how life came about!

Edward O. Wilson, in his book *Consilience* (the unity of knowledge), stated, "Scientists themselves are fortunately not so bound. If past generations had been so deeply reflective and humble before the unknown, our comprehension of the universe would have stopped growing in the sixteenth-century. The chastening sting of the philosopher's tongue is needed, but should be taken with the antidote of self-assurance, and never allowed to be fatal. It is the opposite conviction, blind faith if you prefer, that has propelled science and technology into the modern age. Bear in mind that the original Enlightenment died within philosophy, but not within science. The more pessimistic philosophers may be right about social sciences, of course, but is better to press on as if they were wrong. There is only one way to find out. The more forbidding the task, the greater the prize for those who dare to undertake."

When enlightenment cannot serve, Life will not be.

Pierre Chardin asks the question, "Without the earth could there be man?"

In my method of examining history and pre-history, it possibly would be better to ask the question, "Without man could there be earth?" Although humankind has been the only part of Creation to place themselves as leaders of Creation, one slip, or one mistake on the part of the force that has assembled our great Creation, or perhaps an unforeseen catastrophe by this same force, could cause the annihilation of the human species together with other parts of Creation.

Although the evidence of humankind is speckled throughout the stew of Creation, as yet there are none here on this planet that can expose themselves with the vocabularies that are used by humankind today. Without the operational parts that make speech what it is, and then the assemblage of the miracle apparatus of hearing by which humankind are able to hear other mental abilities, what we see and hear could not be exposed. Without vocal expression, nothing could exist as a definite single part of Creation.

There is no question that humankind desires this force behind Creation for existence. But again, on the other side, this force cannot exist without Creation. And Creation can at this point only accept humankind to be the leader due to their ability to express themselves vocally. Their is only one way in which humankind can feel themselves to be superior. It is not because of the opposing thumb. It has to be the vocal chords and the ear drum that make the real difference.

One must always remember, All Creation sees and listens to the other.

Humankind have argued the fact or fate of time as being positive or an illusion since it was first introduced. The beginning of time came with the beginning of thought. At this or that time dark and lighter were only minute shades of difference. As the Mind's eye was being developed, the appearance of dark and light became more severe. Light finally became true light and darkness followed. The illusionment of the two became a true happening. The word time, itself, is a natural phenomenon that was undoubtedly created by humankind as they watched night become day and day become night. The time it took for light to become dark, and dark to become light undoubtedly occupied our Mind while the All Seeing Eye was buried in the forehead of Creation. As the eyes were assembled and became a possession of Creation, the question of time evolved into a period of time. How to measure it became the question. Many different methods were undoubtedly tried until the shifting sand of the hour glass answered the question. Time itself has never changed, only the measurement, and the different methods of measurement have made it more correct. Still, time as it was is as it is. It is humanity that questions time, not time that is trying to prove itself. Today this definition of time is presented to encompass the universe, yet time itself has never changed. In reality, if we gaze into the atmosphere of the universe at night, it is black; in the day it is blue, or light. As yet we don't fully understand what color it really is. If it is light, it has to be lit up by so many of what we refer to as suns. Then arises the real question. If there were no suns, such as ours, then would it be dark all the time? If this is so, then being in a steady state of unending darkness would present no problem. Time requires comparison. Comparison requires an opposite. Without either of these, time stands still and would require no description.

I will now try to explain something that has, by its own sheer will, constructed itself into Being. The result: this animated matter became from pure thought. And then, through this same continuous effort and self-determination, evolved into a Being which so far is able to realize itself through an explanation to another — the other who stands on the same footing as the Being who made the first move.

In another way, an organ of conglomerated matter explaining to another organ of conglomerated matter the manner in which both came into Being.

If what the scientific world says about the workings of evolution is true, humankind will make a giant step forward in both physical shape and mental conditioning when travel in space becomes commonplace.

We'll know for sure in a short time.

Let's build a campfire, get a tom-tom, and start in chanting and dancing around the fire while sounding the tom-toms and warming up to the hypnotic spell of a trance. They call it performing incantations. Today the computer or television seem to do the same thing. It's a method of releasing oneself. Through this release it is possible to absorb happenings into Brain and eliminate interference of thought. If a person closes their eyes at times, it makes the feeling even stronger.

In ancient times, without television or computer, the Shaman was the instigator of the procedure. The purpose of these incantations were many, but for this particular ritual it was to draw the so-called soul out of a dead body, and then the Shaman would lead the soul to a so-called heaven. There were no questions asked, although I can imagine there were many who witnessed these happenings who felt maybe the truth was being withheld.

How do we know we have what is called a soul in the first place? It's nice to picture we have one, but there has never been produced anything that physically proves that we do have souls. Sole, soul, sool. Alone. Celibate might be the description for this purpose. Celibate describes a sole as being alone — unmarried. Sole could be, and should be, described or spelled as soul. After all, Shamanists would never refer to a sole as being soul, and yet dictionaries cross reference the two in a common manner.

How did we ever acquire a soul? The various religions

seem to make us feel we have one now, and have always had one. Besides this, what is going to represent us when we transpire and transform? If it weren't for our soul, we would have nothing to follow the Shaman off to heaven in. This makes it very easy to convince us that we do have a sole, or soul. To have a sole is easy. Our sole is what is referred to as a foundation, a foot bottom, something to stand on. Also it can cover the entire body. A sole for protection, or a sole to contain our organs.

Also it is referred to as having no sharer, functioning independently and without assistance or interference. Explanations go on and on. Yet, to define its origin, the dictionary says, "Sole-no origin." Soul is different. "Origin - sol, soul, sawol, sela, seula, sawol." They pounded the word soul into all languages. It's a miracle if you don't have one. It's the immortal part of man having permanent individual existence, and it can place itself in paradise, or be consigned to damnation. The ones who decide where you go really need no introduction. It's the same group that tells us who God is and that we have a soul, sole, sol, seula, or whatever else they use to explain something that is not real — or even close to being real.

Man's moral and emotional nature is distinguished from Mind and intellect — a seat of real life, vitality or action. The hidden soul of harmony. All Souls Day is celebrated by singing and begging for soul cakes.

There's only one way that a person can know for sure that they have soul. Death, a word with less meaning than soul, explains your soul leaves your body and is lead to heaven by the Shaman, and maybe your lucky enough to be in the sole. If this doesn't happen, the soul of your body is sent to damnation.

Lately, psyche has been used to explain sole or soul. I don't have any idea what will be next. But I'm sure the religious leaders will be there to present it to the others when it comes.

It's a shame that we have to work around so many fallacies that have been mentally constructed to prevent a clear understanding of what and who we are and our true destiny.

It might just be easier to start over.

If we are to fully understand the beginning of the human species, we must put them in their proper prospective at this time. As to the appearance of matter, this can be achieved by merely looking at our surroundings and taken as truth what the scientists of today tell us. They are able to break matter down to molecules that are the basic parts of matter and conclude that the birth of matter is conceived from electromagnetic friction. The truth is that all substances carried in matter are used in the construction of the unanimated as well as the animated vessels that move in all directions throughout the universe.

Even though the planets themselves are traveling in specified orbits, there are the young, not fully constructed, who wobble and wander as a young child trying to stabilize themselves to be on a definite orbit in the atmosphere of space.

These things, which make up matter, though exaggerated as thoughts, bring us possibly to what is really taking place in life. Yet, birth or generation of new vessels continues. The evolutionary progress of our state of Being cannot escape the re-designing for future needs. When something begins from nothing, it is very easy to change its total appearance as it grows. There cannot be a design accepted today that will be the same centuries from now in our future. The reason being: we do not understand what matter we'll be using as fuel at that time.

One of our greatest problems has been to connect our humanity with a beginning, not through some missing link, rather through the growth of matter which has been produced by Mind.

It becomes very simple when a Being subscribes to the truth that all Being, together with the rest of Creation, are conglomerated matter.

If the electron and the proton are the result of frictional gravitation of cosmotic particles, then they must conglomerate at different stages of Creation to form matter. Matter becomes through this conglomeration of elements — sometimes large enough to be seen by the naked eye. Matter permeates through itself to be any part of Creation. Cosmic order begins with what, for now, we refer to as nothing. Nothing only seems to express something that cannot be seen or imagined, no matter how strong this microscopic energy is.

Again, nothing seems to invite Being.

The way it was, the way it is, and the way it will be are all covered by evolution. Evolution is something we can rely on. It's the way of life, and it makes its plans for life, as life proceeds.

I have in Mind that the word God covers or describes too many things and should be removed from our vocabulary. Of course in other languages of today and those of our historical past, God was and is described by many words with many sounds. Perhaps it would be much better if we made the word God impossible to put down in any form of writing and could only be used or understood as a sound.

Through the church, which tries to represent God, Galileo was given the choice of being orthodox or receiving punishment. This cannot be. God is not punishment, and God does not take choice from anything.

It is possible to place the word God in many positions which require decisions. This is not God being subjected. It is only the word God. It is impossible to place God in any position; God is on all sides and wears no uniform. Even when the word God is used, it desperately wrangles to place whatever It is in a corner. Humanity has forever pressed to be in control of all, including what we refer to as God. With the zillions of vessels who represent humanity, it will be impossible to make a point accepted by all. That is unless money and food replaced the rainfall which covered the entire planet all at one time and was controlled by one Being. (It seems that this happened to a guy by the name of Noah one time.) At this time it could be possible that all would agree to place this Being in the position of being God.

God must be a word with only mental connection or designation. What the word God implies is impossible to mentally be placed in form in Mind. I do not have to explain this thought, because I am sure existence has forever made the attempt.

God exposes Itself in every part of conception. The imagination cannot be used as a means of describing God: God is real.

Where did God come from? God did not come FROM anything. God comes THROUGH Creation. God is and acts through Creation. There is nothing too vast for God to Be. After all, didn't God create it ALL? The force of Creation is undeniable, yet this undeniable force makes every effort to expose Itself in a peaceful manner. Would you not define these actions as the actions of God in a similar orbit?

Where does the food chain start, or let's say as far as we know starts? The cosmos, as far as and beyond Mars, physically are only quaint in understanding at this time. Atoms perhaps could exist on friction or electrodynamics. Elements digest atoms, and organs devour elements. Life devours organs.

Every part of Creation requires a part of Creation for existence. Energy is the gift of Creation. Guidance of this energy remains in the hands of all. Choice is freedom.

Everything is capable of living on something it can acquire, the procedure of catching is up to the chaser. There's no need of me telling about animals thriving on what they are: cannibals. Size most times makes the difference of what eats what. Take only what you need.

Open your Mind, and put your sights on Belief.

Ever since animated Creation has gained eyesight, this sight has presented, besides the glory of the universe, an uncontrollable fear for all that surrounds it. Living only exists amongst others who seek each other as a source of energy, or mutilate one another as a means of control-power. This battle for existence is being fought in every instance of life; it is a battle being carried on in the atmosphere of the planet earth as well as throughout the universe. The battle is seldom fought between enemies, excepting the human race. It is mainly fought for energy, food to exist. Many times the battle is over areas where food or fuel can be cultivated.

Eyesight seems to cause as much grief as it has good. If this possession of sight had never come upon the scene of life, life would have flowed its natural course through existence and made life's journey a great deal easier. Besides the very existence of life, the hereafter would have presented no problem. The question of eternity can be easily answered without the problem of sight. What good would a soul be then? Nobody knows what any body looks like, so why worry about a soul if there's heaven, and we are not able to see one another.

Without sight, no one could realize the physical appearance of the other. The Mind is in complete control, and you could visualize another to look any way you would like them to look.

Birth and death, as I was taught as a child, mean coming into the world and going out of the world. There was no problem with coming into the world. No one really worried about that; you were strictly on the receiving end. However, there is a real problem with going out of the world. Coming into the world needed no explanation, that is only concerned with the birds and the bees. It is going out that presents the problems. First of all, the choices aren't much. There is heaven, where you go if you are truthful and good, and then there is hell, where the devil lives, and if you lie and are bad or commit a sin, that's where you are sent. Sin's a tough one to overcome when they tell you you are born out of sin.

No one has any proof if these choices are true, so why worry? I'm sure there's more to it than meets the eye or ear.

I've spent a lifetime, seventy-six years, reading and listening to stories about a God we must obey, a God we are unable to see. In my younger years, I was taught more ways to fear this God than to love Him. This God, too, was pure male. The female had no right to be considered as God. A few thousand years ago, in some writings, I have read that God was a woman. Woman gained this right by bearing children. It is easy to see how this could be true. When a woman gave birth to a child, at that time, no one had any idea what caused the birth. It was only a fact that they, women, bore all the children.

As progress proceeded through the evolutionary process, the ability of speech developed. Slowly the real cause of birth was disclosed through the observation of nature, and taking into consideration that only the females of any species gave birth through their bodies. I doubt at that early time if any thought was given to the different organs of the bodies, and that possibly the satisfaction of rubbing and putting the organ of the man inside of the woman's vagina brought great satisfaction to both parties. Still, in the early history of man, the causes of birth could not be defined. It could have been through the resemblances of all types of females sex organs that the female organs produced young. Possibly another few thousand years gave them enough time and observation to realize it took the action of the male, in the sexual act with the female, to generate children. When this came about, according to many, man revolted and woman was no longer God. Evidence of this is shown on many of the idols which still stand where most of the noses have been beaten off the statues. Even the Egyptians had female Gods, maybe that's why the nose is missing on the Sphinx. In my travels through Alaska, there was evidence that even totem poles have been abused and the noses broken off of them. The days of female Gods were over.

In my younger days, many tales concerning "our" God were told to me and the other children. It was also explained that to tell a lie was one of the main reasons I would not be able to get into heaven. The sacred gates of heaven, when I was a child, could be closed to me or any of the other children for many reasons. And, at that time, I didn't want to have anything to do with a mean person that they referred to as the devil. There were no reasons why I should believe all of these stories in the books of the Bible. They could not be lies due to the punishment one received by telling lies or even stories. Today I can see that story telling was only allowed to those who were professionals in the religious business. Besides all of this, I made as little noise about religion as I could, and by obeying the rules as much as I could, I would avoid the devil.

My pet rabbits, rats, goats, snakes, birds, dogs, along with my grandma's cat, took up most of my time as a young man. I could talk with them and tell them what I believed, and I knew they wouldn't tell the devil on me. Little did I realize how deep the religious teachings of those professionals was going to creep into my early beliefs. They were always there with their books, or someone wearing a turban, or another that went to a church where they didn't eat meat. They, of the many different religious teachings, were everywhere. The only ones that weren't around these religious teachers were working in the hospital laboratories or schools teaching biology and other sciences classes along with the three Rs, which later I learned to pay more attention to.

As I continued to grow and learn by living in the country (San Fernando, California), I lived very close to nature. I spent as much time as I could playing mountain man. I had two very good friends who were the same way. One of them, Vernon Boston, was raised in South America. He had all sorts of giant beetles and butterflies that came from there, and also some shrunken heads of the local natives where he lived. Vernon could really tell some stories about living in the jungles of South America. Junior Burt was my other good friend. He was a couple of years older and showed me how to wear a loin cloth like the Indians of America wore. By living this sort of life in nature, I was in reality learning about nature that was more interesting than "Noah's Ark," and a God that would send me to the devil for almost anything I thought or did. I felt free.

My study of biology and nature, after about thirty years of "their" God, led me to the study of evolution. Before I took on evolution I read the Bible from beginning to end. My reading went along okay through *Genesis, Exodus, Leviticus* and the rest, until I came to Solomon and the book of *Ecclesiastes*. It was in this book of *Ecclesiastes* that I read probably the most interesting writing. Solomon wrote, "I feel in my heart that God will manifest man to understand that he, too, is a beast. Who knows the soul of man will go to heaven and the soul of the beasts will return to the earth?" This exposed to me what I have learned to refer to as something that allowed everything to go to heaven. Even if heaven was fable. By reading the thoughts of Solomon I began to see that there were two sides to some of the stories in the two books called The Bible. Isaiah took up where Solomon left off in a book of his own. He wrote, "Your new moons and Sabbaths are an abomination to God. When you pray, don't do it on the street corners where all can watch. Go to the closet and pray in silence." I could see now that there was much more to the Bible than I ever thought.

I continued my reading and could now see that there were those who expressed another side to the common understanding of the Bible. This now would be my work. I would profess these parts of the religious writings. I could now read what I wanted to read in my own way, and worship the God that Solomon, Isaiah, and others were writing about. A God of love instead of one that would send you to hell.

Soon, through the continued study of the sciences, I began to feel an attraction to a God I could feel to be there rather than a concealed God who ruined thousands of lives just because they said they "looked upon Him." My God was turning into what I could see, hear, and smell. Freedom was exposing itself slowly to me due to my attraction for nature. I was beginning to realize that others were just as myself. There was no making believe. In fact, over the next forty years, as I continued reading the great works and words of Solomon, Plato, Pascal, Linneaus, Lammark, Darwin, Goethe and many, many others, I began to create a God that contained all Creation in its Being.

Through the studies of the sciences, my Mind was opening up a truth I could believe concerning God. No longer was any God hidden, mean, or not a part of me or the rest of Creation, but just something to fear and worship. My new God was Everything.

I had learned through the sciences that matter could not be destroyed and that all Creation was made up of this same matter. Also I could see that water, when boiled, would drift into the atmosphere and then condense and return to earth as water. I also learned by watching miners pour mercury over earth containing gold that the mercury attached itself to the gold and left the rest of the dirt lay. The mercury was then heated and evaporated through a tube and then it condensed itself back to mercury. The gold remained in the flask where the mercury had evaporated. This exposed me to the facts that matter cannot be destroyed. All metal elements can become gaseous and return to matter. Several elements melted together make up different elements. Science became a fascination and was presenting me with a God I could believe in. This God was Creation Itself. No longer was it necessary to worship something I could not see or trust. Now my God was Life — Creation — Something that could not be destroyed, but a God that made up the very Creation of Life Itself. Not a part of eternity, rather the ETERNITY, of which you and I are a real part.

If some manufacturer constructed the greatest automobile ever created with nothing lacking in conveniences, and an appearance which had never been approached, there would still be those who looked beyond.

When someone explains any object and uses gender to boost its acceptance, they are realistically creating opposition to their explanation. New explanations require middle of the road acceptance first. She or he must be added, if you must, after acceptance.

Fred Schelling, a leading philosopher with German ancestry, states, "Nature is a creative spirit that unites knower and known, progressing together through greater and greater understanding and feeling towards an eventual state of complete self-realization."

When I read these same thoughts by several different writers, it's almost impossible for me to see how close these thoughts are to the truth concerning the answer to our Being. There is no sudden realization, or jump, or instant conversion to understanding the question of existence. Our existence molds together through the flux of intelligence. The word God is a hindrance to our understanding, rather than a support to understanding. So far the word God has been used as a foundation for Being. If the word God is used to encompass all nature, Creation, or Being, and include our total Creation as Being, with nothing excluded, the word in this way passes inspection. However God cannot be used to explain or use as a complete power over our Being.

The closest God, or the word God, can come to explain life is to be a part of the Universal Life. Creation Itself would more than fill the shoes of what we are taught God is supposed to be.

Each of everything is striving to exist. Any method for existence is used to extend this period, even the very instant of digestion of one another is accepted completely as being a necessary method for life.

Mythology has no place in the art of understanding. Beings are placed in the mouth, gnawed up, and then they are digested and passed through the gastric digestion of the stomach to the small intestines where the chyme is digested by the other to become chyle. The chyle is fed to the body which ate the beings in the beginning of this operation, by passing the chyle through the lacteal, who passes it on to the bloodstream through the thoracic duct. This duct is above the diaphragm where the heart, lungs, liver and other vital organs are housed.

Science has proven itself beyond doubt of its vast knowledge of the internal workings of the organs in most matter. In my occupation, in my younger days as a professional hunting guide, I have butchered thousands of "critters," which I am related to, with first hand experience in removing many of these organs.

With the passing of the original Beings through the mouth, the stomach, and intestines to the urinary and anus, the mass of Being (food) is distributed to the body of the Being. A few hours later, through excretion, the remaining, unclaimed excrete and excreta is flushed through the toilet or dropped to the earth.

During this process energy for the body organs, including Brain, which converts its energy to thought through the Mind, is distributed. That which passed through the body and placed upon the earth is in turn digested by those microscopic molecules that exist upon what is furnished them. Not one thing is wasted. All continues through the trail of digestion or food chain.

This process is taking place universally. Thought seems to be the big winner or central benefactor. To some existence and generation are furnished through the permeation or digestion of other Beings. The food chain in actual existence is explained as the "existence chain." The word God could be explained as the existence chain. Humanity is the explanation of those, here on this planet, who lead the process of life. This in no way means they are better or chosen. Rather they are lucky in ways, and yet we cannot fly or live under water, except in airplanes and submarines. And yet we do both as we exist in the other Being's makeup. The MIND we have is the MIND of all. Thought seems to be a result of life. THE CONTINUOUS LIFE OF THOUGHT SEEMS TO FULFILL OUR DREAMS. Humanity is the explanation of those who, here on this planet, lead the process of life through the consideration that they think harder, and more.

It is this thinking or these thoughts that present eternity. Each of these actions along the chain of existence has added ways in which their material bodies can exist. These added conveniences, through the flux of life, are soaked into the reality of life as it enjoys eternity. You are a part of this chain of existence. The methods of becoming a part of this chain of existence are many. No matter the entrance into this chain of existence, it's the continual unfolding, birth and generation where pleasure lies.

That's all folks!

The present exists in the reflection of the past, and the future exists in the reflection of the present: evolution at task.

The same desire to Be guides life. None are chosen, the proven dream on. Believers are there, and nothing stands that exceeds the other. Life gives all equality. Luck provides.

Starvation is the result of generation.

Nothing is nothing. If we have to put up with it, let's relax. It'll burn out! Put up with what you are offered; let them adjust to what you need.

If the genes have the opportunity to be represented in the future, future Creation as a whole, too, will be represented. Here-in lies eternity. If something is represented in the future that exists today, tomorrow will present the same occurrence. Evolution is the reasoning. Mind is Life. The future represents the past as it transforms physically to maintain a relationship with future mentality.

Did Mind create Brain, or Brain create Mind? Once again, Mind over Matter.

Reformation of all matter requires many different temperatures. Conglomeration of these muons, electrons, protons, and neutrons presents a foundation.

The earth's hardest steel is subject to heat. Heat will bring steel to a point of becoming liquid and held at a certain heat the hardest steel becomes an animated liquid.

If heated long enough and hot enough, steel will join the atmosphere.

Frictionalized to present conglomerations, muons, quarks, protons and their electron friends bring about matter: Matter in its earliest stage.

Pure evolution, which harbors all, is the answer to eternity.

Life is an eternal gift to those who exist through the desire to Be. Sleep is the alternative. Both require energy!

The mind is loaded to go at birth. It's almost impatient, yet has to learn the language, be it spoken through sign or tongue. Mind is accepted by Brain as Brain is accepted by Matter. Together they present Life.

An idea would be to figure that God can be understood as Mind. God could be called Mind, they're Both, if you want to figure them that way, after the same thing. I personally feel neither would know what they are without some sort of a language. Mind speaks every language that God could possibly know. If God were Mind, or Mind were God, it is very possible they could and would be the true instigators of what we understand life to be.

I'm sure that if there were something that could exist independently of life, as we know it, it would very much like to talk with Creation. This is what Mind does. It discusses with us, through Brain, Life. The thoughts of all Creation, through Mind, translate to life.

Creation makes reality, and there is nothing more universal than Mind or God.

It's great to Be God, and help others understand they, too, are what We worship.

Brain is conceived in all Creation. Even that which is only considered as atmosphere contains Brain.

Brain is contained in all Creation. If truth be known it is only segregated by mentality.

Consciousness is God getting along with Mind.

Once we open the Mind of humankind to accept the Mind of all Creation to be this same Mind, our next step will be to conclude that this Mind is God. From here we step into the realistic view of eternity.

We must strive to erase from our natural studies that a god has ever had or possessed the ability to conceive and construct the body of man out of clay. As it is today humanity has been created from many materials and matter. All of these must pass through the evolutionary process.

Pioneers in the art of the sciences all conclude that humankind is a direct result of both physical and mental evolution. During the formative era of the evolutionary sciences, bold speculative statements were required to convince others that some animals, or animated Beings, were required to pass or evolve from primitive corpuscles to the stage of standing, thinking, talking improvements: humankind.

If it had been possible for this same intelligence we have today to witness life in the mode of corpuscles being evolved from atoms, it would have been very easy to have connected ourselves to eternity. Animation began when the corpuscles acquired pseudopodia and began to drift and bounce on their false, spiny, velvet legs. Psuedo in its earliest stage meant false. Pseudopodia describes something that is able to move. The eye is able to see the total Being, and able to see that it is able to move in water, and yet the psuedo legs, on which it moves, are difficult to see. Huxley described these as nucleated corpuscles, which throw out very long pseudopodia prolongations. Once again, at this time, if humanity could have witnessed this happening and seen that these corpuscles bounced around in a pool of water in their uncontrolled travel, it could have been possible to attach themselves to eternity. After all, this was all there was to eternity here on planet earth at that time. For an animal which for even a million years to evolve from the atom to be able to move in a direction it desired to go is quite an accomplishment.

Before this was accomplished the closest thing to articulation could have possibly been branches and leaves on the various plants and trees that could have been here on earth at that time. Of course there was water that has been in existence almost forever. If we were only able to examine and watch corpuscles for eternity, once again, life would have been much easier to understand. Although the change from inanimate to animate took thousand of generations, it did occur. During this time evolution was the same process that is taking place today. With or through this process is the same continuous thread of life. Nothing has been lost. The expansion of the thread added elongated animated Beings to the file of life. Just as we see now, through the lens of the microscope, hundreds of different shapes wiggling their way around in a drop of liquid, this same scene has been taking place since animation made its first move.

To come closer to eternity, it must be realized that at one time this scene was the utmost of life on this planet earth. There were no animated Beings larger than those that took a microscope to see, excluding The Universe. Transformation at that time was easy to settle for. What else could there be when another transpired? After all, what other fuel did we have at that time than one another? This was the basic to evolutionized eternity.

As Joseph Le Conte explains, the non-directional pseudopodia body of the gastrula evolved into a longer body and became equipped with a tail. This brought about directional movement with Brain, which consisted of medulla and thalamus. Through medulla came the pulse and circulatory system, thalamus supported senses and, later, smell, and then the optical lobes presented sight, through which directional animation could pick a target through something other than scent.

With the advent of larger and more skilled animated Beings, some of the smaller less important molecular Beings slipped into the background. However, there are still those molecular Beings who are still in existence today and who were in existence when life became.

If we stopped at this point we would have muons, quarks, atoms, corpuscles, pseudopodia and sub-fish who were able to exist and actually travel in a direction that they desired to go. This was quite an accomplishment for only a couple billion years of life here on planet earth.

Once we discover the exact time the beginning of Creation took place, it becomes necessary to understand where, when, and whose idea was it?

It's easy to understand what caused the extinction of the dinosaurs: THERE WAS NONE! There are too many parts of the dinosaurs that have evolved into the creatures of today, to be able to say, "the dinosaurs are gone."

Natural selection seems to be controlled by species. Although all are considered animals, a man cannot impregnate a cow, and a crow can not impregnate an eagle.

Even so an ass can impregnate horse. However, the result, a mule, is sterile. In any case of cross-over the same sterile results apply.

How many times has it been proven that the radical today is the rationalist of tomorrow?

Once again, evolution has to be the true relationship of natural existence.

Just as the progress of physical evolution has forced Creation to physical achievements beyond thought, mental evolution will force the natural sciences, through its general laws, to present Creation an understanding of its Being. As Condorcet asked in 1795, "Why should this evolutionary principal be any less true for the development of the intellectual and moral faculties than for other physical operations of nature?"

Humane is said to be characterized by kindness, mercy, or compassion. Humanism is classed as a system of thought that center on humans and their values, capacities and worth. Humanism is also emphasized as a secular movement during birth of the Renaissance period.

The Renaissance had its beginning, as far as written studies are concerned, during the fourteenth century and continued well into the sixteenth century. This period of time is most known for its rebirth or revival and the transition from Medieval to Modern times. Both art and literature seem to be the highlights of the Renaissance period, however, for the true explanation of the word, one must search out religion as compared to the truth of Being exposed to all Creation.

Humanism seems to be solely an act or display as being the property of humans, which is a direct, incorrect explanation of this very powerful noun. To express this same thought, the dictionary explains humanism as a concern for the interests, needs, and welfare of the human race. If this is only true for the human, why is it that other Beings, including the King of the Jungle, the African Lion, can be so openly merciful to their own kind? Many Beings of Creation show these same signs of kindness to their young, and many times to species of a different kind. I personally watched a woodchuck tend another of its own species with a broken leg and nurse it back to recovery by carrying food to its patient. Some of the food was soaked in water for the crippled friend.

At night the caretaker slept beside the patient. I have watched pigeons feed the young of others, and there is no competition between them. There are many more circumstances in the lives of other animals than humans who display mercy and compassion to other Beings.

I watched a pair of rhesus monkeys in their pen one day. The male had passed away, and the mate had pulled the body to a corner of their pen. After propping the body up in a sitting position the female put her arm around her mate and sat there hugging him. We left him in with her for that night and the next day took him out and buried him.

The word humane has to be spread further into the connection of all Beings. Humanism must include all who display what humanistic values are; this system of thought must encompass all flora or fauna. In fact, even the conglomeration of organs made up of all microscopic bacteria must display humanistic actions rather than being wholly cannibalistic. Humanism has been displayed through all Creation since the Creation of Creation.

The true explanation of the Renaissance period is the separation of science and mystical religions, which guided us during and through the Dark Ages. In truth, evolution is far deeper in humanistic Brain and Mind than the spoken thought of the many mystic religious explanations.

When you eat or have a meal you are feeding the trillions of cells contained in the body, or vessel, you are existing in. The food you eat turns to chyme and then chyle and then dissolves into energy.

When lack of food faces a Being, the food necessary for the energy is supplied from fat which is stored in the body, or vessel, in case of emergencies. Too bad we can't store oxygen.

Once the consilience of knowledge is established, and the consilience brings about the unity of knowledge, we will then return to the dark ages.

The war of minds and mental construction must continue. If any thought reaches the pinnacle of pure reason it will be discarded. To exist we must have the unknown to search through.

If all those of the scientific world become as one mind, advancement would surrender.

If the concentration of the Mind by a human Being is strong enough to cause the head to ache, could it not then be possible for one to be able to concentrate hard enough to create a fire within the body?

Mind is true conceiver of life. When an attempt is made to get to the core of life, in future time, it will be proven that the Mind has always been the creator of life, through thought.

There is no need of self-transfiguration due to the fact that Mind, as your essence, is alive in all Creation.

In other words, if you do not limit your Being to the one body you now live in, and agree with nature that you exist through Mind in the bodies or vessels of all Creation at the same time, as exposed to you in daily life, you automatically come into the eternal existence with an understanding of pure reason.

When any vessel or body succumbs its attachment to Being, IT is not in the least effected. The Mind is what you have been calling or referring to as God. Your explanation of God or any of the many other names you have used to refer to as God has only been used to explain to you something that lives and is exposed through the existence of all Creation. The unending Universal Whole that exists through Itself and contains the efforts of All who play an equal part in this great game of life make up the true explanation of the words we have been educated to use when truly speaking of Ourselves and the rest of Creation. We, as Creation, are the point of existence. We contain one another to prove our existence.

Even the sparrows and their efforts to help in the continuance of life, as pleasure, are contained in what it is that gives us Eternity.

Existence can't be referred to as time served here on earth. Also, Existence is Eternity. Birth can only present Eternity; there is nothing else.

Creation is most often mentally looked at as a happening of the past. Creation as fact is in control of eternity. It now appears that there is no possible means of destroying Creation. Creation is matter in all forms. Matter is CONTINUAL. It can't be destroyed. True, it can be dissolved in different manners. However, dissolution in any way merely presents matter as another part of Creation. Transformation of matter may be achieved through heat, cold, subtraction, or addition of atoms to its structure. Creation re-acts through evolution for the survival of Itself, which describes the finite to the infinite. Creation might be thought of as the Great Controller. After all, Creation is God's manner of exposing Itself too Itself. If this were not true, how would life know how to express the correct manner in which to exist?

Birth, in most cases, presents the act of the sperm (male) penetrating the ovum (female). Polymerization results in a chemical reaction in which two or more small molecules combine to form larger molecules: reduplication of parts in an organism. A molecule can be explained as the smallest particle of an element or compound capable of retaining chemical identity with the substance in mass.

Gamete is identified as a mature germ cell possessing a haploid chromosome set and capable of initiating formation of a new individual by fusion with another gamete. A germ cell reflects as an egg or sperm cell or one of their antecedent cells.

Taking into consideration the previous information concerning birth and the make-up of the to be born, just as other explanations of science, will reflect new information as evolution unfolds. Our benefits at this time are that now we have a foundation to build our theories on.

What starts the spark of life will probably result in a phrase we now use when the thought of birth enters our minds as, "The spark of life." Generations of the different species are produced in several ways, yet the enclosure of the nucleus in most instances is protected by what we now know as egg. In its earliest use the word egg was coating or tissue, in other words, covered with egg. As time presented itself, a future egg became the hard covering of the nucleus born to animals including turtles, snakes, birds, and other reptiles and was the most protective method of incubation during the period of the dinosaurs. On the other hand, the egg of the human species after unaccountable time became known, after parturition, as "afterbirth." Yet, while the young of most mammals are being formed, they are contained in tissue commonly referred to as the egg sac. In most mammals, those suckling their young, the gestation period takes place with the young enclosed in a tissue (egg) inside the female parent. This might be considered as an improvement over having to incubate the hard-shelled egg or eggs by sitting on them for long hours keeping the temperature just right for hatching.

The method of impregnation of the female by the male, when necessary, takes place by different methods and in several ways. However, through observation, basically all require that spark of life which in most cases comes from the friction of the Beings involved. In the case of birds, strutting or strumming seems to create the sensation of concentration which brings about electromagnetic friction. When the correct time presents itself, the mate hops on the back of the squatted female and, as their sexual organs touch a spark, much as a spark builds in your body when you walk over carpet, presents itself in the sexual organs as they touch. This amounts to the ejaculation of the sperm of the male into the ovum of the female.

Study of the sexual acts of most other animals can be plainly seen just as with the birds. However, in every case friction is undoubtedly the direct cause of the generation of the electromagnetic friction necessary for birth, or the "firing of the cell."

Further study might present the splitting of the single cell during birth similar to the power of concentration of dreaming when a human Being is possessed by a wet dream.

Impregnation and its scientific interpretation will undoubtedly flow through many streams, and the positive cause will still be doubtful. However, birth by the side of death presents two thoughts that may never be fully understandable. The greatest explanation of either will still contain an etheric view. Even today they question others of the human species who have undergone what others try, in vain, to pronounce as death. Death invites more liberal circumstances of an understanding than birth. Birth is tightened from disclosure, more so, by the period of time when the born are able to speak, and what the words are capable of disclosing at that time through the understanding of those who are exploring their meaning.

It was three-thirty this morning when I suddenly awoke and a thought came to me. This thought, I am sure, came to me as a result of reading once again Ernst Haeckel's book, *The Evolution of Man - Volume II*. My thoughts, as many know, are to promote the relationship of humankind to all Creation through the satisfaction of intelligence. No longer to put the human Being on a mythological pedestal that presents the human race as being superior to other Beings of Creation. For me to do this, it has been essential for me to conglomerate all Creation into a mass of matter that is lead by one inclusive Mind. And with which this Mind is a psuedo-connection to each Mind/Brain of every member of Creation from Haeckel's indescribable moneron to all members of the human race. Mind, in all actuality, becomes One when any situation presents the Mind/Brain. Mind is a secure part in the mental make-up of All. Mind Itself is Celestial. Mind/Brain uses Brain as a psuedo-connection to Mind.

If this is true, then evolution has spent Itself, and there will no longer be any change or development. Nothing could be further from truth than what should and will take place in the future of Our Universal Creation. Many changes are instantly going on within the total sphere of Universality every instant. Most of these are not able to be seen, as they are either too small or too far off in Universal Space. Food-energy will not always be what it is today. Food-energy in case of a great change will make the many vessel bodies of all Creation evolutionize more so than any other reason. Remember this. It took billions of years to get to the top of the tree, and we haven't hardly gotten started!

This thought that awoke me this morning involved the pedigree of man, as drawn similar to most trees of life, as viewed by most scientists. Haeckel's drawing of a large, burly oak placed monera at the root of the tree, and we can settle for that, and man at the tree peak, as I have said before. From monera at the root, an assortment of names of cells, worms, nettles, ascidians, amphioxus, reptiles, ganoids, animal, mammals, bats, apes, and finally, as I said before, man at the very top. It seems that if anything was going to be at the top it should have been God. Over fifty listings of creatures who lead, or furnished evolution a foundation from the first monera Being, Matter, to the human race on top.

I admire Ernst Haeckel for the effort he has exerted while attempting to explain in every way possible what we really are, a conglomeration of matter that seems to be alive. Even with all the efforts of this great scientist, time has only presented to us another answer to the question and understanding of life. Just as the Wright brothers' first flight has lead us to space and also visiting the moon, the evolutionary trail is steadily unfolding new and adventuristic thoughts to the Mind. This thought which awoke me last night may add to this evolutionary unfolding.

Mind, a word or etheric Being, which I have chosen to replace the name God, has been with Us since the conception of thought. To Be, to live Life Itself, has exceeded all desires of Being. Now, with a foundation, life, due to the length of Its time, has presented Being with a problem. Life is too short! Why is it that we have no understanding of the real period of life? Life must extend into Eternity. Why should Something spend billions of years creating the human race and then only let them live a few years? It looks like we've only been created to be buried, and heaven is where all the action is, or earth is only a preparation for heaven.

Perhaps this misunderstanding has been forced on us by the several ideas we have settled for that have been offered by others of our race. There have been many mistakes made by many Beings including those which have been furnished us by Mind. These mistakes have taken us to many abrupt endings, causing our return to start over again.

In these over fifty specified names, which Haeckel has listed on his tree of life as Beings, are some that have existed and then become extinct yet still exist in the Mind and bodies of others. Brain, due to its meaning, is one noun I can accept as forever being the operator of any type vessel or body Mind decides to create to exist in. If monera, at the root of Haeckel's tree of life, would have settled for the name Mind, and all animals would have settled to be called Minds, we would have been able to see that all are creatures of Mind moving through the process of evolution towards greater productions of life. None are truly different than that which exists now. True, the matter is the same and the Mind is the same; it's the physical appearance and the color that make the only difference. Mind is eternal through Being. The confusion is brought about by assuming all require names, when in reality they are all the same, Mind is always Mind. Maybe it's easier by using names. However, confusion is brought about when names are used to disclose identification. A name only adds to the problem of feeling different. Bob, George, Betty, Jim, etc., seem to be okay. The reason being they are chosen at random. Lion, horse, mouse, etc., are designated or regimented.

If for instance Haeckel had started at the root of the tree by saying Mind as monera, Mind as amoeba, Mind as worms, Mind as dinosaurs, Mind as birds, Mind as apes, and finally Mind as Man, it would have given us all an attachment to ALL CREATION rather than just man to man or monera to monera.

Mind is Mind, or God is God, or Deities are Deities. Names mean nothing, and many times are only confusing. They have only been a means of making it easier to identify something, and I'm positive we really need no name to explain to all of us what each other is. Yet, by using names, it separates us. We and everything are all a conglomeration of matter for eternity. Each protects the other, yet each mentally and physically digests the other. None are above or below the other. All are presented life, not as a gift, but a duty. Mind, God, or any other name that covers US ALL, will lead the way.

It's much easier when we realize that we're all the same in material and mental make-up. Physical shape presents the problem.

Mankind, with their evolutionizing of the automobile, might be compared with the super desire of what we explain as God as Creation continues to unfold.

Getting down to the nitty-gritty: it is really God who likes to ride in cars, and God's the one who's behind all of the comforts that are added to each new model. After all, God lives through mankind, and all the rest of It's Universal Creation.

Perhaps God, as Mind, in another part of the universe, has developed Creation to the extent of higher understanding.

We should prepare ourselves for the future; not continue to argue over the past.

Accepting the proof of both physical and mental evolution does not remove the prospect of a Heaven upon transposition. Rather it presents the knowledge of a Heaven at hand. Eternity, as fact, belongs to ALL. By acknowledging the fact that each is a part of all, the word "death"is uselsess. Not a disappearance of either, merely change. The actions of All creatures are instilled in those who visualize the life that surrounds them. Life holds truth for all Creation. All Creation digest benefits from others. Life brings about relationship, relationship has no boundaries.

We exist in others as well as existing in ourselves!

The final sentence in Walter Black's introduction of *The Works of Francis Bacon* expresses the kingdom of Eternity. The words, "Bacon the man went down into the dust with Essex three hundred years ago, but the words of the writer still live." Many of my attempts to explain my feelings concerning eternity have fallen in the same dust Black placed Bacon in during the early sixteen-hundreds. However, my chance to raise both Bacon and my explanation from this dust have been presented to me by Black.

All Creation serve the purpose of Life as material Beings in our Universe of Matter. In so doing this service, there are none who have either wasted or sacrificed this period of Being. Each, through Life, have produced a variety of efforts that have been used by others who are also passing through this same lifetime duty. Life is a duty, and the fulfillment of this duty is presented to the jury of Being who, as they live, sift through them and live by the useful. Bacon is far more alive through the actions he displayed than due to the writings he constructed. His accomplishments have far exceeded his writings. Proof of this is in the notoriety he was exposed to during his time on earth and the effects he produced.

This same materialistic view can be considered by all who have existed on the plain of life as the Universe continues to unfold Its future. All existence, since forever, has left their mark on the registry of life. Our reward is created for us through our past as we continue to uplift Creation. From the smallest to the grandest actions of any or all of Creation affects this plan of life. The desire has and will always be there to display life, which contains a make-up of all actions which Creation has passed on to eternity. Nothing misses the scrutiny of all that are here, in the future and in the past. Every event shall be passed on to the eternal which consists of all that are and will be living life. Everyone and everything that is or will Be form and add to the foundation of existence. Our mentalities are the same mentalities that grope continually throughout the Universal Mind for ideas concerning our Being. Being is living, and living is furnishing experience to those of our future. Experience is the flux of intelligence. Our indulgence by accepting what others offer in life before us are the endowment of eternity. To live life amongst those who continually are, and through accepting the duties of investigation by the single force of desire, eternity presents Itself in a milder form every instant as Life lives on.

Eternity is surrender. Surrender by mentally accepting oneself or any other part of Creation as Being under the guidance of All. Not only are the written words of Bacon with us today, his very heart and mind are even more elaborate as are the thoughts and wishes of all Creation who have added the abilities of their existence to Our Bank of Eternity.

It could be possible that this same prehistoric evolutionistic process has taken place many times prior to our sprouting up here on earth. It is also possible that the mental strength of Mind over matter has been producing physio-mentalities billions and billions of years previous of any type activity here on planet earth. Perhaps even before earth became.

With each new batch of the evolutionary physio-bodies with mental abilities and as many planets that are able to accept them, the story of production has varied due to the incapability of the Conceptor to produce like to like. Again, it is probable that the substance of Ourselves and the rest of Creation make up this Conceptor and It's impossibility of being unable to formulate the exact same shapes of physio-bodies or like to like repeatedly. Again, it is most probable that the mental abilities of us as Creator lies within Creation, which factually involve each other in making up what I see as a Universal World of Creation.

Therefore it is my exact opinion that Life Itself is the Progenitor of Our Universal World. Common sense proves that All Creation, of which man is a small part, is born of Itself. To grasp Eternity there is no other way than to lay hands and mentality on All that have and still do exist in our formula for life.

TO BE ETERNAL, ONE MUST BE A PART OF ALL.

Before any Being, animated or unanimated, is able to subscribe to the order of eternity and feel whole-heartedly to be a part of this Universal Eternal Matter, they must include themselves into the eternal make-up of all life. As this life presents Itself, All must automatically be included as a part of each other. For fact each, no matter their size or appearance, must know themselves to be the other. Let harmony replace judgment.

To remove mass by neutralization is, at the present time, one of science's priorities. First you see it and then you don't would be a reality. Scientists know what it requires to do this, yet intelligence at this time has no answer as to a way to bring about conglomeration after neutralization.

When this does come about through mass neutralization of a body, or Being, those who perform the operation will understand by being a physical witness to the action of what has taken place.

The more difficult problem at hand then will be to put repolarization in effect and reassemble the same Being back to mass in the same shape.

They say all of this requires a soul. I feel a *sole* would serve the purpose better in this case...

The sole's not in my way any longer. From here on out it's clear sailing.

Who needs a heaven?

Aggressive Beings create their own competition!

Muon seems to be a lepton that appears to be almost identical to the electron, except for being unstable and having a mass about 207 times greater, and is the chief constituent of cosmic radiation at the surface of the earth. Originally called a mu-meson, but now no longer classed as a meson.

What next?

Carl Sagan, in his very good book, *Cosmos*, states, "We're here and they're not, when referring to Beings of past history and pre-history."

By reading my writings it is easy to see my disagreements with Sagan's thought. We are all here, now! Every being ever born is represented in the house of Mind/ God, Carl Sagan's even more.

The Mind of Being and the Spirit of Life are but forces that are inseparably connected with each molecule of the material substance which make-up the bodies of Being. Just as the motive force of our flesh is involved in the muscular form-element, so is the thinking force of Mind involved in the construction of Brain. Our Spiritual forces are as much functions of this part of the body as every force is a function of a material body.

This is as true of inorganic natural substances as of organic. In entirety Mind connects to Being, no matter Its shape or size. Mind fills atmosphere more so than Being.

Man can assemble a radio from the parts that they have manufactured. Mankind then plugs it into the electricity they can produce, and the radio will pick up the signal from an amplifier they also put together.

So far man has only learned to repair the organs of natural Beings and make it possible for them to continue their lifetime of reception from Mind. At the present time humankind are only able to experiment with constructing a human heart. How long before they are able to manufacture and assemble human parts remains only a guess.

Mind is only a realization of what it really Is.

The flux of Life generates immediately as Mind connects with Being at the time of conception. Being, during conception, requires information for survival. Mind, in Its ethical state, must furnish this information in order that it may complete the process of Being for Its own benefit.

Medullary acceptance can be proven as the inspirational bank. Medulla is, once again, the source, power, and force of Life. Medulla provides the first breath and voluntarily puts the circulatory apparatus into action. The umbilical chord supplies matter for energy. The future places the mother in charge of nourishment, and Mind, through medullary reaction, will supply organization.

At conception the flux, life, establishes the connection of Mind and Being, and the embryo sparks Life. Mind can only continue to develop. This is a decision of Its own. If this were not true, Being, a product of Mind, would cease to Be. Mind can only survive through Its production of Life. Life is proof of Itself.

Women become more women-like each day, while men merely sit by and realize it.

Soon physical strength will have served its purpose as a means of protection.

Women boxers are improving.

Mind developed matter through atomic reaction. Protons, Electrons and Neutrons, which all contain Mind, swirled in frictional motion attracting and repelling each other until the correct recipe formulated itself into Matter. A substance in which Mind is able to continue its existence and conduct Itself while fulfilling Its dreams.

This existence that matter furnishes Mind as a home had in reality, through rationality, become imprisonment. Mind had ultimately constructed a mass of matter in which to exist without having complete control. Life was now an unending decision.

Through this assemblage of energy, Mind, without realizing the results of Its desires, has caused the birth of ultra-mundane, an equal to Itself which must be tolerated for both to Be.

It's up to Creation, as always, to realzie its position.

If what Joseph Le Conte explained is true, medulla is the inner substance of an organ, which is pith of the plant or marrow of the bones. This seems to be the essence of the relationship of plants to animals.

Containment of medulla is not limited as pith or marrow to plants and bone. Medulla is also explained by others who tell us medulla oblongata is a widening continuation of the spinal chord, forming the essential part of Brain and containing nerve centers that control breathing and circulation for existence. If this is correct, the spinal chord is the container of medulla just as the plant stem. Oblongata in its own rights merely explains something as being oblong. Therefore medulla oblongata is an oblong form at the upper tip of the spinal chord that is the base of Brain. Just as the stem of the plant contains pith (marrow or medulla) in its stem and grows the flower (head) of the plant, the spinal stem contains marrow (pith medulla) and grows Brain (head) on its tip. Both the stem and spinal chords are containers. Medulla seems to be some trace element held within a fibrous container that is able to receive transmissions from Mind to any organ which contains medulla; this could mean liver, heart, kidney, etc.

Evidence proves that each organ is contained in its own sole or vessel/body. In the case of humanity, and many other animals and inanimate Beings, all organs in each of us contain medulla in their make-up.

Waking up a single cell is very simple. Now I can

understand why animals, with all of their organs, are so difficult to wake up! It's kind of like saying, "Let's strike up the band."

It might also be considered that if the tip of the spinal chord at the bottom were stuck in a flower pot containing the correct substances, then the spinal chord would bud-out brain just as the stem of a flower does.

In the early 1900's Ernst Haeckel wrote, "Man is not above nature, but in nature." Carl Sagan, in the early 1980's, wrote, "Our obligation to survive is owed not just to ourselves but also to that cosmos, ancient and vast, from which we spring." He ended his book *Cosmos* with the simple, yet great, statement, "We have always been space travelers."

Haeckel also stated, "The whole knowable universe forms one undivided whole, a 'monon.'" Even though his word "monon" lost its value as a word (undivided whole), it still stands as truth. Humankind are still as much a part of nature as they were in Haeckel's or Francis Bacon's time, or even when we were, or as we are, Cosmic Rays waiting for the planet earth to be constructed. And, as Carl Sagan says, "...and we're still space travelers." The planet we have been traveling on for over fifteen billion years has neither lost nor gained much speed; it is still traveling around the sun two and one half million kilometers every day. When Carl Sagan wrote, "and we're still space travelers," he is undoubtedly referring to ourselves who continually travel through space as passengers on earth, and rays from cosmic life.

Billions upon billions of years have been spent, if you want to consider time, in our evolution through Cosmic Personalities and organs, to the vessels we are wearing today. It is incomprehensible to describe the thousands of shapes nature clothes humankind and the rest of Creation in during our evolutionary climb. All of nature is processed through this same series of events, and all of us, as we spin on our global space ship, are still heavily involved with this same procedure. To keep up with this, we must continually check with our past as a reference to our future. Our past history, including our traveling as Cosmic Rays, are possessions we will always hold. Every Being that exists carries thoughts that are valued during life in the Cosmic Ocean as our planet earth swirls.

To open oneself up mentally, and to be able to accept All Creation as Being a part of what we feel ourselves to be, is very difficult. It is much like surrendering to others what one feels to be their prize possession. While in reality each is losing nothing and gaining all. To feel yourself as you, and you alone, is depriving oneself the benefits that are included in feeling yourself to Be a part of Creation. By only having humankind as an equal part of oneself, and humankind by one way or another exterminated, all connections to Being humankind are removed, and it would then be necessary to begin over, and this time join the others of Creation; a position we have and will always own.

By resigning to Be a part of All Creation it is impossible to have to start over in any case. Matter, as we understand now, cannot be destroyed. Matter can be changed but never lost or vanquished in any way. Through this fact the physical bodies of Creation will be forever in one form or another and join as One. Through this statement comes eternity for the vessels of All Creation, no matter time. By surrendering oneself to Be living through All, All at that instant automatically presents Itself to Be forever as Matter is conceived as One, and matter is what we are. As proof it is very easy to see that our minds connect to Be as One.

Mentality travels this same course. Mind, through its construction of Brain, has succeeded in the composition and fabrication of a physical Life; All are naturally nature in which Mind exists. Mind IS through Creation just as matter is Creation. Nothing can escape existence even as seed is germinated. Existence through the flux of life supercedes all. Nothing is lost or able to perish. Gain is Life's only sequence. All information, which concerns Being, is reflected through the intelligence of Mind. Mind has been, and will always be the true beginning.

Mankind, along with all Creation, have been connected to eternity since the conceivement of Life. All are made of matter; all consume matter and breath matter as atmospheric life. All are connected to the materialistic make-up, which unfolds through the evolutionary process of desire. Mentality is furnished through Mind, which leads the course of Creation. Each vessel of All Creation is a contributor to the laws of nature and is alive in the matter, which beholds Creation. It is impossible for anyone or anything to exist without existing eternally.

Being's daily duties are reflections to the evolutionary process of Being. Each of these reflectionary duties are digested by Life into the future of Being. This future of Being represents in total what has taken place through Life to the point. It's impossible to Be without presenting gifts to our future. Eternity belongs to existence. Existence is forever a sign of Life in an easier mode.

Mankind is not the only species who were or are trying to push their intelligence into a future. First the single cell had to develop pseudopodia in order to move. Then the fish must learn to swim in a chosen direction. Then the fish must develop wings and learn to fly. The amphibian then had to learn to breathe an atmosphere with less density in order to leave the water.

All of these accomplishments, although achieved, are not the completion of our Universal Evolutionary Process.

Space is a whole new ball game. And, when terrestrials appear, remember, "It's only me, from over the sea," said Barnacle Bill the Sailor.

Carl Sagan wrote in his book, *Cosmos*, "To learn a little about what other kinds of civilizations are possible, we can study history and cultural anthropology. But we are all of Us - Us whales, Us apes, Us people - too closely related." He continued, "As long as our inquiries are limited to one or two evolutionary lines on a single planet, we will remain forever ignorant of the possible range and brilliance of other intelligences and other civilizations."

I might say in opening, I will never be able to repay Carl Sagan for his efforts involving the enlightenment of humanity and the other parts of Creation as to the results evolution has furnished in making our lives more pleasant and much easier. Not for some perhaps, but his intentions, I am sure, are for All.

Next I'm sure the many fans of Carl Sagan will argue my point. However, I have no other way to see humanities' relationship to All Creation.

When Sagan expressed Us while writing, "Us - Us whales, Us apes, Us people," I'm sure he was referring to the relationship of humanity to the mammals. Many before him have used these same similarities of birth and then using the breasts as the humans do. If this is true, what about the thousands or perhaps millions of years before we stood? Or even before this, when we swam the seas? When did mammals first appear? Before we were mammals, when we didn't even know humanity existed, whom were we related to then? Back to the same old story, "I don't know, but I do know we're chosen." Nay, as they said in the mid-eighteen-hundreds when a "divine spark" was supposed to have been breathed into Brain of all mammals, not only are we NOT chosen, we have never, nor never will be chosen. We stand now as a part of ALL Creation. Our brother's walk on four legs, some with fifty legs, wings, they slither, they swim, they grow leaves and needles, and many of these other creatures are our greatest friends. They are Us and We are they. This relationship will only grow better.

I can only hope our relationship to All Creation is better understood before we do encounter, in real life, another from a far off planet who looks different, speaks different, and thinks different. After all, difference still hides in the eye of another.

By understanding now our total relationship to one another our future becomes brighter. This kinship, by degree, will bond slowly through the flux of life. Soon Creation will discover that by the experience of living our eternal connection to each other becomes stronger. The fabrication, which will bond Creation, will expose Itself through Mind, something we can prove ourselves through, and Be.

Rene Descartes, 1596-1650, has been called the father of modern philosophy. Rene radically distinguished between the Mind, perceived as indubitable, and the body, explained on the basis of purely mechanistic principles.

By distinguishing Mind to be perceived as something indubitable, Descartes stated Mind to have the quality or state of being unquestionable. By being unquestionable, Mind is indisputable, accurate, certain and faultless. Surely looking at Mind in this manner could only include a part of it, in the same way we examine Brain. When a person speaks their Mind, they certainly are not indisputable, accurate, certain or faultless. In fact, in many cases it would be just the opposite. However, Mind on Its own can certainly prove Itself to be indisputable, accurate, certain and faultless.

It's when the tongue waggles that Mind gets into trouble. Before the tongue waggled, Mind had control of Itself. The problem came when creatures started speaking to one another, "In their own mind."

Even a dog can get in trouble when it barks!!

However, we must continue to cast our thoughts and receive our dues.

If I, as a Human Being, were able to concentrate, concerning my Being, and it's dissolution through the flux of Life, both in and out of existence, I could feel myself to Be included.

If I were able to see and to feel the organ in which existence proves me to Be, as a flesh and bone machine, under my mind's complete control, my Spirit would be exhilarated, even overjoyed.

When I am no longer able to retain this control, my Spirit wanes.

For Life it is a requirement that the Spirit rise and wane, just as the heart and lungs inhale and exhale.

Life is eternally passing through the process of resuscitation, both physically and mentally.

All life exists on the same raft.

Those who are asked to decide, and are unable, will tremble.

Those who volunteer, yet do not perform, create the faithless.

Those who do, yet don't believe themselves, will perish through dissolution.

Those who decide, and feel faith in their decisions, are digested into the tablet of life.

It's possible that the rebounding reflections of Life have more to do with the natural evolution of Being than the spoken words or sounds.

Each of Creation's Beings, seen or unseen, animate or inanimate, casts reflections. As a whole these reflections can be considered as intellectual messages.

Digestion of these, by others, no matter the species of each, are the true directors of Life.

Before in my writings I have mentioned the word 'descent' as being used by Charles Darwin and many others in describing the ascent of man. At the time of Darwin many never realized the real power of the Old and New Testaments.

In studying both of these books a person sometimes gets the feeling that Being was not really supposed to have happened. "We were conceived in sin." This sentence is a real blow to anyone who is reading these books to feel better or have their Spirit lifted.

When Noah was told by his God that He, God, was going to destroy all Life on earth because they were bad was another blow.

Once again, Isaiah's God told Isaiah He was going to take the world and turn it upside down and shake all life off of it unless they changed there ways — another blow.

Descent in the dictionary is described as, "to move from a higher to a lower place; come down or go down." If I were a broad-minded person, I might just take Darwin's words, THE DESCENT OF MAN, as climbing down out of the trees and becoming human, instead of being ape-man and living mostly in the trees. Darwin, I am sure, knew what word he was using when he gave or described the title of his book as, *The Descent Of Man*.

The descent of man could still take into consideration Adam being made of clay by their God. By using the word descent, Darwin might be doing just as their God had done.

Descending could have placed man in a state of going back to dust instead of heading for space.

In reality, Charles Darwin was tracing humanity back to its roots. During the period in which he was writing, he was comparing mankind to the gorillas or apes, which was quite a problem. And then to DESCEND millions of more years to the time of Dryopithecous was beyond belief. It was here, in the mid-eighteen hundreds, that we became aware of an unaccountable missing link that has never existed.

Dryopithecous, so far, remains our earliest fossilized evidence of being bipeds. For our intelligence to descend further, we must relate to THE ORIGIN OF SPECIES, of which we are all a part of.

Sagan comes close to Spencer, who first stated the earth was constructed of Universal atmospheric particles. Sagan stated in *Cosmos*, "The earth condensed out of interstellar gas and dust some 4.6 billion years ago." After Spencer, who in the middle 1800s made a near same statement, mythological tales presented the exact construction of the earth and the Universal Heavens in many ways. One had the Great Designer molding planets in his hands out of clay and throwing them into the Heavens. The truth of how and when the formation took place will be argued for many years to come. At present, unless we get involved with immaterialism, we know it did come about, and we are here with the rest of the Cosmos to prove it.

The progress made since its conception presents the earth itself, prior to the Cambrian period, as being covered with a condensed liquid defined as water. I have never read a thought concerning whether the water entirely covered the earth or not. Sagan speaks of the Cambrian explosion. This explosion presented the planet earth with vast supplies of all kinds of flora and fauna. Undoubtedly the flora, in the beginning, consisted of algae either in the water only, or in the water and on the land. Again, fauna could have existed in either and have, after passing through the basic evolutionary stages, infested the planet with an unending supply of insect life. This acidic insect population, without doubt, was an unlimited source of food for the plant life.

By the time these insects had evolved along with the giant reptile population, the earth must have produced an over abundance of food to those who devoured vegetation. These results were large vegetation devouring reptiles (dinosaurs). Right by their side, and undoubtedly devouring the vegetarians, were the flesh eaters who became giants by being supplied with this same overabundance of food that was passing through the bodies on the vegetarians' side of life. These monsters, it seems to me, literally ate themselves out of food only to become smaller through other physical shapes in evolution.

True, in the first billion years the planet earth passed through the stages of hell as it boiled first as a swirling mass of molten plasmatic magma, and then through the cooling process became coated with a covering of these same elements. As this process continued, the crust shrunk becoming a large, brittle-like covering which cracked and rumbled with volcanic reactions. Passing under and over each other for millions of years, the plates continued adjusting themselves into the future of a solid mass which would eventually support Creation. Not completely over, this yawning and spurting of magma, this same process continues today with it's shattering earthquakes, which are the results of these same plates grinding against one another.

No matter how long or how hard we seek information, mythology will never produce the answers we are looking for. Perhaps we will lose many of these mythological stories we have based our foundation on, but science will ever so slowly move closer to proving our beginning. Science today has far out proven and presented an unestimated amount of benefits to the health and pleasures of life. Mythology is very lacking in these same benefits. At most its presentation of benefits has been limited to holidays named in benefit of mythological characters and those who conceived them.

It is a very sad situation concerning the grip religion presents to control some of civilization under the fear of a God that will not reveal itself, and yet is displayed as being able to hold all Creation, including the cosmos, under its complete control.

If Mind didn't make mistakes, we wouldn't have misformed Beings.

Even the Great Groper sometimes get caught!

Mind is a force in Itself that is involved in All Beings. These Beings throughout the Galactical Universe, both organic and inorganic, and either animate or inanimate, must contain Brain. Brain possibly could be the initial investment of Mind/God. This force of Mind/God could have only desired to Be, no matter the design. In other words, any Being, in order to exist, must have enough intelligence to receive thoughts from Mind/God, which ever It might Be. The simpler Being, the simpler Brain, and the shorter the basic message required for life. Basic intellect is a necessity. Every Molecule of every material substance which makes up any cell or organ must contain the basic material of Brain or medulla. Medulla, basic Brain, produces the force of circulation and the breath of life, as promoted by Mind/God.

Just as this force of motivation, medulla, a title we will use now, is involved with the muscular operation of circulation and breath, it is also entangled in the operational mechanism of the complete organ through Mind/God. Medulla, or whatever may be the future title, is also the child or responsibility of Mind/God. So too is this same force to Brain. Brain has never been limited in operation until after it has received a full compliment of its organs. Medulla, as we know it now, is the organ of breath and circulation, as I have said many times before, and is self-contained until Brain finds itself in need of other organs. Brain in the organ blastula seem to be satisfied with medulla. Brain, in the sub-species of pre-historic times, eventually constructed through the evolutionistic procedure presented by Mind/God, the thalamus that added senses to Brain in cell life. However, Brain today is contained in all Beings, yet is limited to organs according to requirements.

We seem to be unable to study Mind/God as we have Brain. Brain is physical, Mind/God seems to be in the hand of philosophy. However, without Brain the mental force of any body would or could not exist. This might take us back to the point that without Beings or Matter/Creation, there could exist no Mind/God. Brain, no matter it's ability or size, is our prize possession. The first in thought by Mind/God must be Brain. Brain has to be the primary physical Being or organ of life. When any force manifests Itself in the material mechanism of an organ, either animate of inanimate, the order must pass from Mind/God through Brain, the receiver/transmitter of all physical life. This same receiver/transmitter is contained in all Beings with more or less organs, never with too many or not enough. Beings are a physical force of matter and mentality. Matter may come in many sizes or shapes. However, we now understand Brain must be housed in a container. As the knowledge becomes greater, Brain must enlarge. The greatest display of this was the enlargement of the skull of the human species when speech and the memory of words came into effect. We must keep in Mind that Mind/God is etheric, meaning it contains no matter in it's make-up. Mind/God flows through the atmosphere and Beings as the flux of Life. Beings must receive instigation to be.

Upon transpiration of the sum total of a Being, dissolution cancels the force of conglomeration, or frictional electromagnetism, and the sap of existence evaporates. Automation immediately puts every organ cell on its own stability to receive orders directly from Mind/God with Brain as needed.

During this time of life, before transpiration, a Being demonstrates life. Any and every moment of this Being has been recorded in the flux of life to be used as experience in OUR future Beings, and presents to Us a better method of existence that Mind/God has striven to exhibit ever since the idea of life first presented Itself.

This Idea, from nowhere, now exists together with ALL matter and Mind/God.

Mind/God, although being etheric, continually receives glimpses from every cell or organ in the flux of life's past to secure and enhance the future.

As Mind/God and this flux of Life fill the Universal Atmosphere, these glimpses might come from any direction, at any time, and from anywhere in our vast world of space.

It is possible Brain has organs that were before medulla, just as the atoms we know now contain quarks and muons which are a connection to Cosmic Rays.

Mind/God could have only been interested in Brain "in the beginning." Brain could have been the "one" who wanted to see and motivate itself in the creation of a vessel to exist in.

Even though dogs are considered as man's best friend, there are still many tribes today who consider them as a meal. Possibly the methods used to acquire the meal is the reason.

As these nomad tribes pass over the lands, their pets, dogs, are allowed to run free. The dogs are forced to supply their own meals except for the bones or whatever is left from the bare carcass of the dogs used to feed the nomad tribes.

These dogs might have the motto, "leave the running to us."

It beats cannibalism!

Today we are surrounded by so many different sounds city life is beyond description. In the wilderness the silence is suddenly overcome by the shot of a rifle or a jet aircraft breaking the sound barrier.

Imagine ten thousand years ago. The crack of lightning as it streaked across the sky and then followed by the rumble of thunder. Or perhaps the rolling sound of an earthquake as it shakes the ground around you. Sounds were very limited and none were continuous, thus barring the unheard sound of the sphere, earth, as it spun along its orbit through space.

At this time music, melodies, or the association of any mental sounds undoubtedly settled the organs of our bodies. Musical tones undoubtedly came from our mouths just as the tones produced by whales, birds, coyotes and wolves, or as the wind as it whistled through the tree branches. It seems that almost anything gave off some sort of sound. The Crow Indians were named Crows because of their copying the sounds of the Crow/ Raven.

For some reason we of earth seem to be sheltered from the vibrations and lyrical sounds of earth, moon, venus, mars and the rest of the planets as their continuous paths circle us. The Pythagorean Scale is a result of these sounds. The Master, Pythagoras of Samos, writes Pliny, had the gift of hearing these tones of the planets. Many ask, "is the Harmony of the sphere a poetic conceit or a scientific concept?"

Others have delved into the facts of harmony. The harmonious sounds set up by twin engines on a racing kart, to my ears, accomplish for me what the spheres do for Pythagoras and the rest of us animals.

It has been less than one hundred years since a part of the white-race, who classify themselves as scientists or philosophers, have allowed the black-race to be part of THEIR CLAN: humanity.

Some of this clan have today now allowed a selected few of the bipeds to join their club, while some of the others, more advanced, have allowed all of the mammals to be registered as part of humanity at this time. In fact, even the birds can join. Bipeds are defined in most dictionaries as any two-footed animal, and that's what a bird is.

How long must it take before these chosen ones will realize the rest of Creation also belong to this same flux of Life, which gives ALL CREATION the Spirit of Being.

Mind is slowly teaching those who lay claim to God that God's only means of existence and display is through CREATING, no matter the design, or color.

What fools we immortals Be.

We had better be careful and, "not put all of our eggs in one basket." If it is true, and I feel it's not, that man came along after Creation had passed through the dangerous, yet vigorous flames and explosions during the period of earth's formation, and landed in Eden, then we'd better beware. Through the thoughts of many, man seems to be a late-comer. Showing up after all the rest of Creation had already built a foundation that would stand for man to start out on, and then lead the rest.

It's reasonable to understand that if this is true then perhaps man will drop to the status of the rest of Creation, whom we are now taught to be above, and another Being will come on the scene who will not be congenial to man, and there goes all we've worked for.

It's much better, and safer, that we join the rest of Creation now. And realize what we actually are merely an equal part of Life's existence. None are under, none are over.

Conceived through the frictional spasm of sexual orgasm a Being sparks to life and gratifies Itself with energy supplied through the umbilical chord. A hurried process of evolutionary growth produces child.

Brain came to Be just as body, and was excited through thought by metaphysical forces of Mind/God, and world appeared, sense digested odors and the eyes absorbed first sight. Time was first recognized with the revolving of darkness and light. Sound slowly became recognizable through repetition.

Soon heat became a fact as well as cold and joined darkness and light. Sound was an ability that would be educated to speech. Hearing would surpass mutters, and movement would become standing, walking and running. Life's possibilities were expanding. Everyday of life became more educating and more exciting.

While these evolutionary processes were proceeding, others who Became were absorbing every action and reaction just as this child was observing them. Observations seem to be the foundation of life and prove to be a method of offering the Brain something intangible to digest and approve and then sent forth in thought for all Creation. Learning expanded as observation presented a continued melody of sounds and actions.

All of these rewards are not merely reflected through humanity; they produce themselves to be taken advantage of by all Beings of Creation, whether Micro or Macro. Life threads and weaves Itself in many ways in forming matter,

Being. Experiences are the reward for all, just as growing and learning. All of these are absorbed and digested by Mind/God as a means of unending evolutionary improvement both mentally and physically.

As these methods of life continue, and the peak of Being is reached, receding replaces growth. All of these actions and sounds of every Being, no matter shape, size, material make-up, or color is recognized and memorized through passage from Brain to Mind/God. Nothing passes through the attention of Life without being absorbed and digested. Both of these processes take place in every Being concerned with Life. The Beings themselves are those who exist through, and are the force of, an intangible Mind/God.

Upon termination of our beginning as a form of Our Mind/God, we are able to see the value of our Being. The World of Life that has surrounded every Being proudly exposes benefits produced by All who have existed. None have lived, or existed in vain. All anxiously await the future of Our History, as the Charity Ball continues.

All of Life remains Life as Mind/God. This World of Life constituted as Mind/God inundates the entire Universe. All pass through the evolutionary process and become another improvement of what was before. Every animation, as It is supplied from conceivement, is molded into the betterment of Being. Every Being that ever Is, still Is through their absorption into this flux of Life, Mind/God. Life is the only process of Life.

Eternity is a thought developed — which until now has been a question.

The immortality of Being is found in the Creation of matter as Life. The immortality of Life is guaranteed as Matter Being. Matter gains Its immortality of Being through generation.

As long as Both Are, Both will Be. The loss of either will cause the loss of Both.

To Be immortal, one must only exist.

If we were to use existence as the first principle of Life, to Be, Life would then border on reality. Life, just as any of the many ways used to describe a Creator, is unexacting. There seems, at this period, no exact way of describing Life, or something responsible for life. This situation or condition has confronted all Creation since Its conception. With no direct connection to Something that has no identity and really is not known to exist as fact, the human race has become explainable as the planet earth's major contortionist. Many possible explanations conceivable to date have been exposed in an effort to present proof of a deity that gave us existence. This existence, Life, has always been ours no matter our size or shape. However, to those of Creation who only exist less than a summer afternoon, our span of life as humans seems okay. But when something like the planet earth is explained as fifteen billion years old, our lifetime seems less than a summer afternoon. Besides this, if my or your time is less than one hundred years, why bother us?

Consider this: Our first step back into the history of our past might be to picture ourselves without auto-motion. No rockets, no airplanes, no cars, no trains, no type of locomotion other than our physical body, just as it was one-hundred thousand years ago. No wheel, just on foot or floating on a log. Take away another thirty-thousand years from our prehistory to this situation and it could be possible that we were without clothing, possibly we only had fire. Take away another million years and it could be that our bodies lost some of the physical characteristics we have at this time. The human race with the loss of another two million years could have forfeited all traces of humanistic appearances and thought. Our mental abilities were on a par with a Creation, which only had the desire to Be, and just as today to Be in as easy a way as possible. The future was not. It was for All at that time rigorously only an attempt to exist.

Again, at this time our Mind made little attempt at improvement; improvements only became through desire, which was brought about by natural happenings.

As we continue in reverse we fade into a thing that only existed for a short summer afternoon. Yet we were what we still are today, a part of Life. Once we were without references. Today we're still part mosquitoes. Distinction was inconceivable. At times something else caught and devoured you while you were busy chasing your own meal. Energy was only existence. Generation was only a spark.

Today consciousness has provided us with the power to search through the past and to recognize by diagnosis what I have attempted to explain as a condensed version of how Life has presented Itself to All Creation. Conception has never or will never be presented as a steadfast physical property. Upon conception a Being is offered the opportunity of adding to the sphere of Life. Even though the process of extinction continually digests what has been, the energy received promotes a physical and mental future. It is inadmissible to feel or believe anything or anyone who has passed through the process of Creation to not feel themselves to be a part of what All have, as a whole, conceived. Neither thought nor matter can be wiped from the slate of Life once It or they have lived — no matter for how long. Digestion is always followed by improvement.

Eternity, like all thoughts, must be for ALL. Life is a continuation of Its own reflections. Something that has been Seen by others will never cease to Be.

It was made possible for Creation to be able to feed and exist on dry land by the atmosphere who fed the soil to create lichen.

You came out of what was originally conceived as nothing: the atmosphere.

You stand together as bodies, machines of flesh and bones, created for the sole purpose of carrying ME, your God/Mind, about as I search for methods which I can use to improve you or your design, and make it easier for ME, your God/Mind, to exist.

We are what We really want to Be for now: That's what really matters!

We must soon accept invisibility to be a major part of our existence. Friction now seems to be the only source to expose the results of the unseen, and yet there have been forever tales, which include unforeseen happenings. Possibly lightning in the sky is used most for an establishment of the fact that something appeared out of nowhere. Many times I have watched a high peak in very cold weather as the wind from the north blows against the north side of the frozen peak, which is covered with snow. As the breeze continues, condensation sends a continual stream of the condensed air southward on the opposite side of the peak. As the process continues a great cloud is formed and sent on its journey.

Again something out of no-where.

In ancient times our ancestors, who gazed on these same peaks, at the same happenings, undoubtedly witnessed this same cloud-forming action. Many times, in all probability, some could have seen the formation start from nothing. This allowed the witness to enhance what they had seen and relay it as a work of the Gods.

Most instances of happenings of this sort in our prehistory were declared to be actions of the Gods. Today we see these same exact happenings and settle for what they really are, a Chinook wind blowing along the back side of a frozen peak and condensing the frozen wind from the opposite side of the peak.

Just as we now see truth in what is miraculously happening in our spatial atmosphere, other solutions will present themselves in our dream world of unseen events. Once our mind receives a solution to an occurrence, it seems that solutions bring about solutions. As we are addressed with these, we mentally become stronger and stronger as we understand the causes, and what we used to classify as a miracle becomes factual.

Our greatest example of this sort of situation is now known as common birth!

What I can't really believe, in this 21st century with the education our young people are receiving via television, how it is possible for the story of Noah's Ark expected to be true. While they search Mt. Ararat for Noah's Ark, with no success, others are finding fossils millions of years old. I have a terrible time trying to expose, or dispose of Noah's Ark as being truth. On my desk in front of me is a trilobite, which is approximately 500 million years old, if you want to take "time's" word for it. Otherwise it might be a minute ago, and our lifetime is only a snap of our fingers.

A look at nature will present life as it is. Worries are not caused by nature unless man, as a part of nature, brings about problems of his own.

Because of the unlimited size of our planetary system and the regularity of the cycles of our own galaxy, many are receiving answers to questions they never asked.

Noah seems to bear impossibility, just as others of all religions are teaching what they don't understand.

God told me that if they don't stop telling all of these mythological stories about how it began, He's gonna shave our planet and turn rain into salt.

Phaedo came so close to unraveling the question of God when he stated, "While in the company with the body, the Soul cannot have true knowledge." In other words, the Soul cannot control the body and has only the hope that It, as Soul, will outlast the body and carry out the duties of getting to Heaven and the afterlife at the side of God.

If Phaedo would have replaced God with Mind and Soul with God, he could have made clear his statement: WHILE IN THE COMPANY OF THE BODY GOD CANNOT HAVE TRUE KNOWLEDGE. In reality, Mind, or God/Mind if you must, has to rely on a delicate kinship with each organ of Creation, especially humanity. It's not exactly like we have been taught as written in the good books. God has to work or exist through Creation. Humanity, while in good health, something that God enjoys, has learned the value of morals. Humanity also understands today, through the former explosions of the "A" bomb, and many, many devastating wars, that they must not listen to leaders who desire power through war. This is the greatest wish of the Mind that God is and lives through while in the Body of Man.

If the truth be known, it is just like Phaedo says. While in the body of Creation God is fine; it's in the body of humanity that God enjoys life most due to the luxuries humanity has created through Mind. Again, it is in the body of humanity that God/Mind loses control. The delicate kinship with humanity becomes more delicate each instant as humanity gets closer and closer to a full or complete acknowledgement that the life of Creation is the incarnation of God/Mind.

Proof of this has not nor will possibly ever be written or spoken. Mind can only glance the subject. God/Mind envisions a Creation to exist in and with. Humanity became, along with all Creation. The fire of life God/Mind kindled can only be restrained by stopping the disasters humanity has continued to implement on themselves. Overcoming these dilemmas will present Creation, including God/Mind, to live truthfully and eternally as the Body of ONE.

God/Mind absolves the desired actions and intelligence of All life as It continues to store these in Its vault of Life Eternal.

Conception furnishes each Being who serves as both producer and conceiver.

As long as we have different Gods, We'll never be able to have peace.

God/Mind is Creation; Mind leads the way.

There's nothing better to exist on than what you're made of.

We are, As God/Mind, a cannibal of intelligence.

From where Creation arose, God/Mind has Its Sanctuary. In turn God/Mind continues to actualize Life through the aesthetic atmosphere to a point of ecstasy. No end can be imagined, just as origin has no reflection.

While Here it is most worthy that We understand our close past and near future. As tangible, God/Mind presents Creation as Life to All. Each of matter, yet none identical either mentally or physically, none are given power over the other. All are as One, yet exist separately. Creation presents Life as the process of evolution progresses. Only intelligence and actions are retained by God/Mind.

On Becoming, through conception, We are presented the gift of Being and the force of Life. Another place to house the God/Mind, no matter the size, shape or color. Through this Being God/Mind will accumulate greater senses for the future Creatures of Our World Universe as All serve Their part.

As Creation, All Life exists in perpetual progression. Each present their benefactions, which in turn serve to better the future existence for All.

Just as birth, the sequence of continuation of Life is interrupted. Disintegration serves its purpose. God/Mind must continue as other Conceptions, while atomization devours what was, and God/Mind embraces the value of All who continue to exist within the One Mental form of God/Mind for Its Eternity.

Homer's Golden Chain is explained by Marcrobius in the Middle Ages, and authored in print by Arthur Koestler in the middle of the 20th century, "the attentative observer will discover a connection of part, from the Supreme God down to the last dregs of things, mutually linked together and without break."

It's impossible to put humanity in a special or chosen position in the words of wisdom that Homer spoke. And it's also impossible for a flea to give birth to an elephant. Dreg, as Homer referred to it, was the smallest thing imaginable. God/ Mind must Create from the vaporless vacuum of thought. The lowliest things must Be first. The problem We have today, and which has always confronted Us, is what is the lowliest dreg? A temporary answer today might be rays from the Cosmos. It seems as We see now that the largest things We are able to realize or recognize are the sphere-like bodies of the planets which are scattered throughout our Universal World. Through the explanations of science, We now understand the formula for matter in most cases. We are far superior in our discoveries from what was understood at the time of Homer, 1000-800 B.C. The force of gravity, as well as electromagnetism come from nowhere, cannot be seen when two objects are rubbed together. This same process will cause fire or heat first. If this magnetic force is to begin, it produces a magnetic force that is aetheric. We cannot consider it to be matter. However, to keep rubbing presents heat that will eventually present smoke and then sparks and fire are given birth. The same results might be considered when lightning takes place among storm clouds. Fire seems to come closest of all Creation to Being classified as matter and yet cannot be held as physical. The best one can do is photograph fire. You can shut your eyes and put your hand over it and it will burn you, yet it is not really there.

If We took Homer's Golden Chain of Life and turned it around to read, "the attentive observer will discover a connection of parts from the first dregs of things up to the Supreme God/Mind, mutually linked together and without break." This process Becomes into effect from the Golden God/Mind as a thought and grows to be a desire, which in turn Became. Through the static friction of disturbed thought, which drew heat, just as concentration makes Brain ache, pain conceives matter. The lowliest dreg receives Life. From this point, through the evolutionary process, Creation Became in Its lowliest form. Truly not seen, however THERE!

It comes to Mind that possibly lust could have furnished the energy.

The greatest part of Our Mental Eternity is created through those who spend their lives searching for Its source. No matter the results. It's fact a coin has two sides, just as a thought needs proof.

Ella Fitzgerald sings, "I don't know where I'm going, but I know I'm going." Ella's vocalizing, I'm sure, will carry her far into the future where We All are given the priority of what is Eternity.

My mind is so open it houses the universe.

Conclusion

Once dissolution becomes active in any conglomerated cell-like organ, vessel, or body, the identification of that Being is set free. However, not one part of this Being is lost, nor has any transformation or transfiguration taken place, To continue, only the spoken or written name remains as a reflection of that Being. Just as the former physical shape was made authoritative through Birth by conglomeration, dissolution presents this same state in reverse during termination. Every molecule of matter returns to its own circumstance. Nothing is physically lost. All experiences, including thoughts of this particular Being, are retained in the flux of the Mind of Life, along with the method of birth, conglomeration, and dissolution. We are well aware that dissolution is brought about in many ways. Some are instantaneous, and others may take years. All result in the same climax -- loss of Being in a physical manner.

Loss of physical Being has no effects on the results of experiences which take place during Life. Mental Life continues as It always has through the Mind of Life -- the ultimate achievement being understanding.

Mentality expands and tempers Itself with every experience presented during Life. This mentality of every Being infiltrates Itself into the flux of Universal Intelligence and Thanksgiving.

Eternity is a gift of Life to All. The first breath cannot escape foreverness, just as the last breath adds another experience. All experiences place their full value before Life. Life is the evolutionary process of what so far Lives and continues to Be: a part of the Mind of Being. Eternity's only value is experience. Life without Being can be compared to Being without Being: an impossibility. True Being does not require matter. Matter is used only as an impersonation of proof. Existence is the vapor of Life.

We dwell forever as the Mind of Existence: Being. Birth, as always, presents the opportunity. Dissolution represents the perpetuation of Birth.